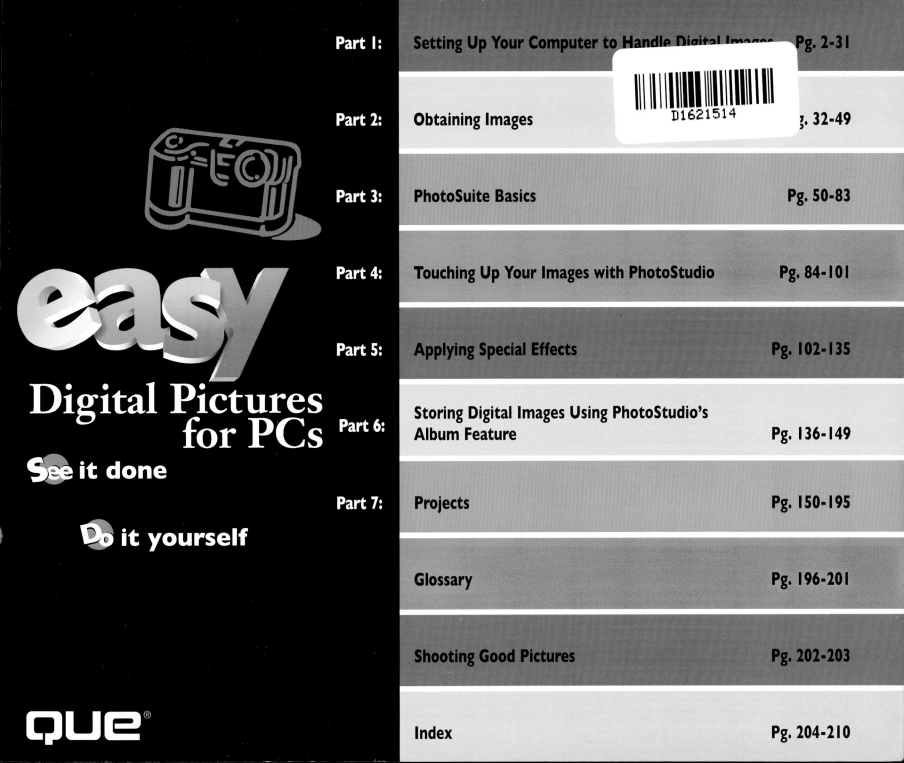

easy
Digital Pictures for PCs

See it done

Do it yourself

que®

D1621514

Associate Publisher
Greg Wiegand

Acquisitions Editor
Christopher Will

Development Editor
Sarah Robbins

Managing Editor
Thomas F. Hayes

Project Editor
Karen S. Shields

Copy Editor
Julie McNamee

Indexers
Aamir Burki
Sandra Henselmeier
Christine Nelsen

Proofreader
Jeanne Clark

Technical Editor
Robert Patrick

Team Coordinator
Sharry Gregory

Media Developer
Jason Haines

Interior Design
Jean Bisesi

Cover Design
Anne Jones

Copy Writer
Eric Borgert

Production
Dan Harris
Cheryl Lynch
Jeannette McKay

About the Author

Kate Welsh is an editor and freelance writer/photographer who lives in Indianapolis with her husband and her dog.

Acknowledgments

Thanks go to Joe Runde of Kodak and Tara Poole of Shandwick for supplying me with a Kodak DC240 digital camera (a great little camera!), and to Tracy Smith of ArcSoft, who furnished me with ArcSoft's PhotoStudio and PhotoMosaic (I LOVE that program). Also, thanks to Jason Haines, Chris Will, Greg Wiegand, Sarah Robbins, Karen Shields, Kay Hoskin, and Julie McNamee, who helped me get this book out the door.

Finally, I would like to thank my father for buying me my first "real" camera when I was 15, and Josh Kantor for teaching me how to use it.

How to Use This Book

It's as Easy as 1-2-3

Each part of this book is made up of a series of short, instructional lessons, designed to help you understand basic information that you need to get the most out of your computer hardware and software.

Click: Click the left mouse button once.

Double-click: Click the left mouse button twice in rapid succession.

Right-click: Click the right mouse button once.

Pointer Arrow: Highlights an item on the screen you need to point to or focus on in the step or task.

Selection: Highlights the area onscreen discussed in the step or task.

Click & Type: Click once where indicated and begin typing to enter your text or data.

 Tips and Warnings give you a heads-up for any extra information you may need while working through the task.

2 Each task includes a series of quick, easy steps designed to guide you through the procedure.

Drop

Drag

How to Drag: Point to the starting place or object. Hold down the mouse button (right or left per instructions), move the mouse to the new location, then release the button.

1 Each step is fully illustrated to show you how it looks onscreen.

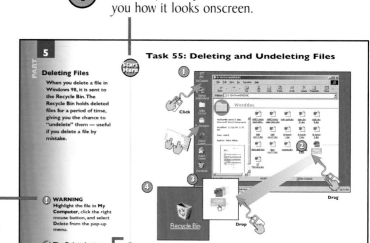

Task 55: Deleting and Undeleting Files

Deleting Files
When you delete a file in Windows 98, it is sent to the Recycle Bin. The Recycle Bin holds deleted files for a period of time, giving you the chance to "undelete" them — useful if you delete a file by mistake.

WARNING
Highlight the file in My Computer, click the right mouse button, and select Delete from the pop-up menu.

The Delete button
Highlight the file in My Computer and click the Delete button on the toolbar.

1. Click the **My Computer** icon on your desktop.
2. In **My Computer**, key in **my file** the file you wish to delete.
3. Press and hold down the left mouse button and **drag** the icon into the **Recycle Bin**.
4. Release the mouse button to drop the file into the **Recycle Bin**.

3 Items that you select or click in menus, dialog boxes, tabs, and windows are shown in **bold**. Information you type is in a **special font**.

Next Step: If you see this symbol, it means the task you're working on continues on the next page.

End Task: Task is complete.

Tell Us What You Think!

As the reader of this book, you are our most important critic and commentator. We value your opinion and want to know what we're doing right, what we could do better, what areas you'd like to see us publish in, and any other words of wisdom you're willing to pass our way.

As an Associate Publisher for Que, I welcome your comments. You can fax, email, or write me directly to let me know what you did or didn't like about this book—as well as what we can do to make our books stronger.

Please note that I cannot help you with technical problems related to the topic of this book, and that due to the high volume of mail I receive, I might not be able to reply to every message.

When you write, please be sure to include this book's title and author as well as your name and phone or fax number. I will carefully review your comments and share them with the author and editors who worked on the book.

Fax: 317-581-4666
Email: consumer@mcp.com
Mail: Greg Wiegand
            Associate Publisher
            Que
            201 West 103rd Street
            Indianapolis, IN 46290 USA

Setting Up Your Computer to Handle Digital Images

I know, I know. You're ready to get right down to business with your digital pictures. But here's the thing: Digital images and the software needed to manipulate them can be real memory hogs. You might not even have room for everything on your computer! Plus, you'll want to get your monitor set up properly and install some image-editing software. So, before you dive in, take some time to tweak your system—you'll be glad you did!

Tasks

Task 1: Determining Available Disk Space

Before you install the software required to view and manipulate your digital pictures, you might want to get a sense of how much available memory your computer has.

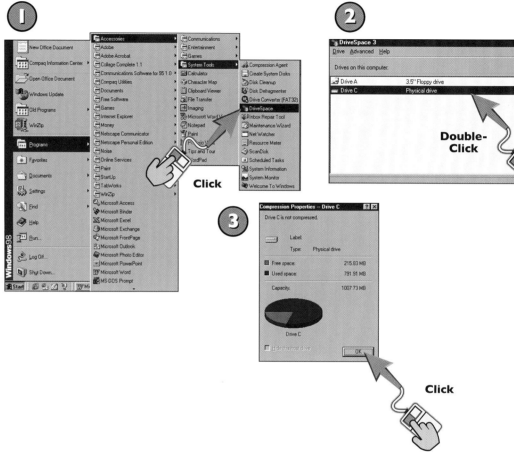

Click

Double-Click

Click

✓ **Piece of the Pie**
You should have a minimum of 100MB of free space at all times; otherwise, your computer will slow to a crawl.

1 Click the **Start** button, choose **Programs**, select **Accessories**, click **System Tools**, and choose **DriveSpace**.

2 In the DriveSpace 3 dialog box, double-click the entry for your physical drive (in this case, drive C).

3 The Compression Properties dialog box indicates how much space is currently available on the physical drive. Choose **OK** to close this dialog box.

Task 2: Using Disk Defragmenter to Speed Up Your Machine

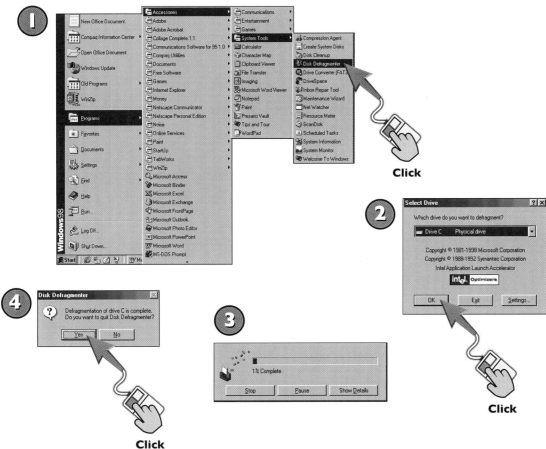

Click

Click

Click

Think of your hard drive as being like an ice cube tray that is partially full. You set the tray under the faucet (a file); when one partition of the tray becomes filled with water (data), the excess spills into the next partition. If the next partition already has an ice cube in it, the water moves on until it finds a partition that is empty. In this way, the data in a single file can become fragmented, meaning that when you try to open that file, your computer must search hill and dale for all its components. Fortunately, you can defragment your drive, restructuring it so that each file's data resides in single (or adjoining) partitions. This can greatly speed up your machine.

1 Click the **Start** button, choose **Programs**, select **Accessories**, click **System Tools**, and choose **Disk Defragmenter**.

2 Select the drive you want to defragment (this should be your physical drive—usually drive C) and choose **OK**.

3 The progress bar indicates the progress of the defragmentationk process. This can take awhile; go do some laundry or walk the dog.

4 The defragmentation is complete; choose **Yes** to quit Disk Defragmenter.

End Task

Task 3: Deleting Unnecessary Files from Your Hard Drive

Start Here

Graphics files—and the image-editing programs you'll use to manipulate them—can be real memory hogs. To make room, you might need to delete files that you no longer use from your hard drive.

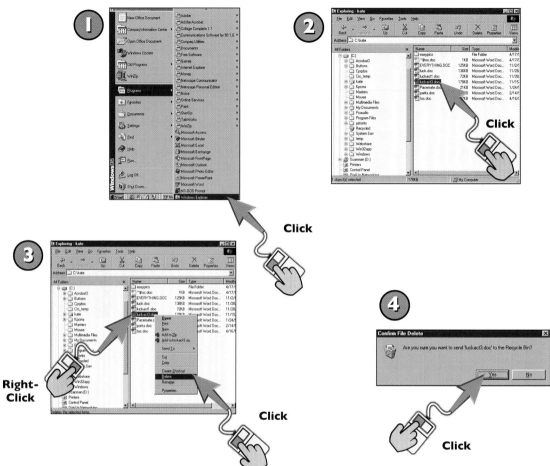

① Click

② Click

③ Right-Click   Click

④ Click

✓ **Uninstalling Programs**
This task covers deleting files, not the programs that create them. To delete whole programs, you should *uninstall* them. See Task 5, "Uninstalling Programs You No Longer Use," to learn how.

① Click the **Start** menu, choose **Programs**, and select **Windows Explorer**.

② Click the file or files you want to delete.

③ Right-click the selected file or files, and choose **Delete** from the shortcut menu that opens.

④ In the Confirm File Delete dialog box, choose **Yes**.

Next Step

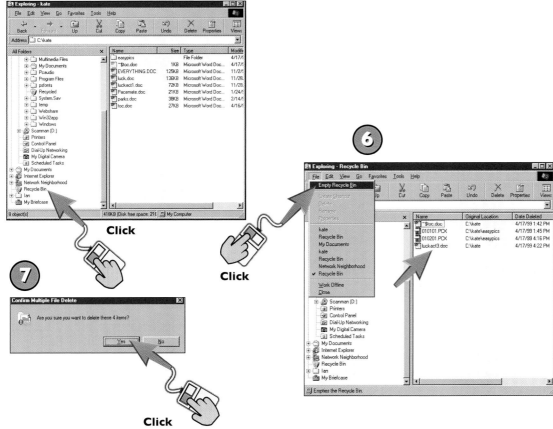

Click

Click

Click

 Recycle Bin

⑤ In Windows Explorer, scroll to find the icon for the **Recycle Bin**. When you find it, click it.

⑥ Deleted files appear in Explorer's right pane. Erase these files from your drive by opening the **File** menu and choosing **Empty Recycle Bin**.

⑦ You are asked whether you really *really* want to empty the Recycle Bin; choose **Yes**. The files are erased from your system.

Recycle Bin
Just because you've chosen **Delete** from the shortcut menu and confirmed the deletion doesn't mean that the file you're trying to delete has disappeared from your computer. Instead, files you delete are first sent to the Recycle Bin. To erase the file or files that you're trying to delete from your hard drive (thus freeing memory), you must empty the Recycle Bin.

Task 4: Deleting Files Using Disk Cleanup

A fast way to delete certain types of files from your machine is to use Disk Cleanup. With this tool, you can delete your temporary Internet files, other temporary files, the Recycle Bin, and program files that have been downloaded by Internet Explorer (such as ActiveX controls and Java applets that are downloaded automatically when you view certain Internet sites).

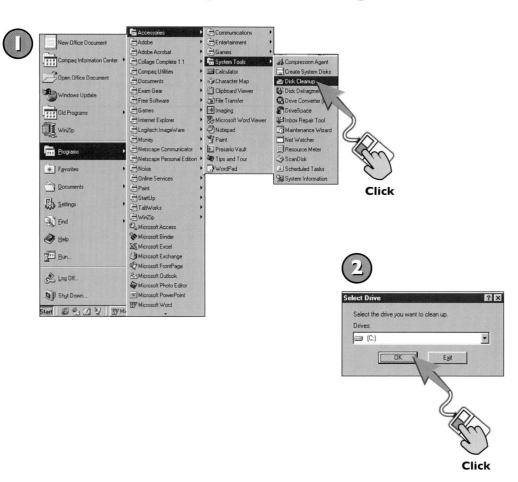

Click

Click

1. Click the **Start** button, choose **Programs**, select **Accessories**, click **System Tools**, and choose **Disk Cleanup**.

2. If the drive you want to clean up isn't shown in the **Drives** field, select it from the drop-down list and choose **OK**.

Click

Click

Click

Click to select the types of files you want to delete (it's probably safe to select all the entries on the screen)and choose **OK**.

4 Choose **Yes** to confirm the deletion.

5 A progress bar indicates the progress of the deletions. When it disappears, you're ready to go!

More Options
Click the **More Options** tab in the Disk Cleanup dialog box to find a few buttons that might prove useful. For example, you can remove any Windows components that you don't use, and uninstall programs you don't need.

Page
9

End
Task

You probably have several programs on your computer that you no longer use; now is a good time to get rid of them. Deleting programs is different from deleting files; to delete programs, you must use the **Control Panel**.

Task 5: Uninstalling Programs You No Longer Use

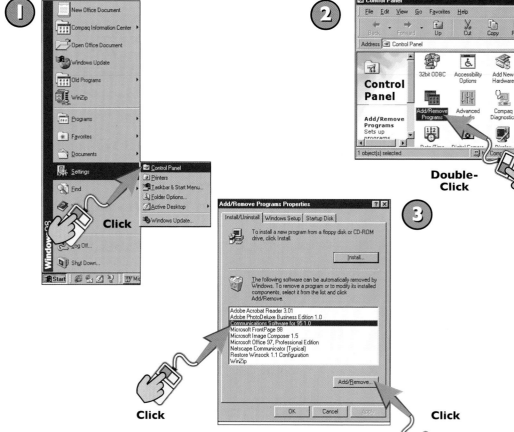

Double-Click

Click

Click

Click

1. Click the **Start** button, choose **Settings**, and select **Control Panel**.

2. Double-click the **Add/Remove Programs** icon.

3. Select the program you want to uninstall, and then click the **Add/Remove** button.

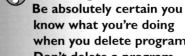

Next
Step

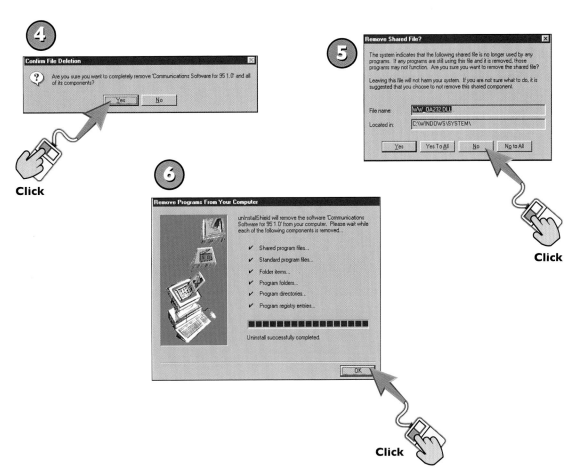

Click

Click

Click

④ Confirm that you want to uninstall the software by choosing **Yes**.

⑤ You might be asked to confirm that you want to remove various shared files. If you're not sure, choose **No**; you don't want to remove files you might need for other programs.

⑥ The program will be uninstalled from your computer. When the uninstall is complete, choose **OK**.

Task 6: Configuring Your Monitor for Best Viewing

Your monitor can be adjusted to better display your digital pictures. For example, you can alter how many colors your monitor displays (the more colors your monitor displays, the more lifelike your image appears).

✓ **Available Colors**
The number of colors available to you depends on what type of monitor and video card you have.

✓ **How Many Colors?**
How many colors you decide to use depends on what you plan to do with the digital picture you're working on. If you only plan to view the image on your computer or place it on the Web, 256 colors should suffice. If you plan to print the image, select more colors.

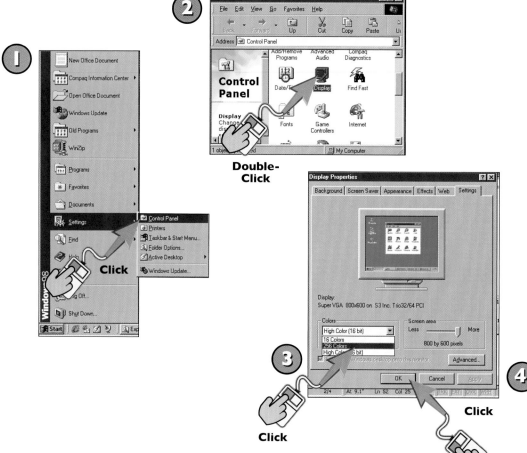

1. Click **Start**, choose **Settings**, and select **Control Panel**.

2. Double-click the **Display** icon.

3. In the **Settings** tab, click the **Colors** drop-down list and select either **256 Colors** or **High Color (16 bit)**.

4. Choose **OK**.

End Task

Task 7: Creating a Folder to Store Your Images

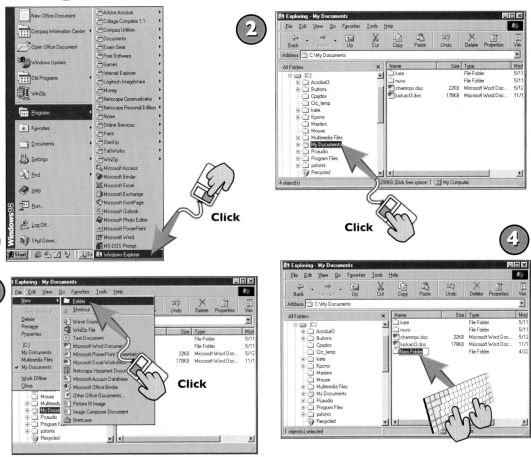

Storing your images in a centralized location is a good idea; that way, you don't have to root around your hard drive to find the images you want to work with. I keep mine in a subfolder of the My Documents folder; however, you can keep your images anywhere you want.

Click

Click

Click

① Click the **Start** button, choose **Programs**, and select **Windows Explorer**.

② Navigate to the **My Documents** folder, and click to select it.

③ Click the **File** menu, choose **New**, and select **Folder**.

④ The new folder appears; type a name for the folder (whatever you like), and press **Enter**.

Before you can print your
digital images, you'll need
to connect and install your
printer. (If you've already
done so, feel free to skip
this task.)

Task 8: Connecting a Printer to Your System

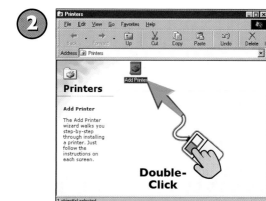

Double-Click

Click

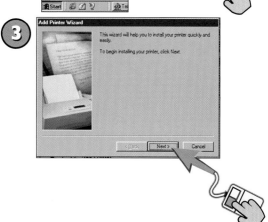

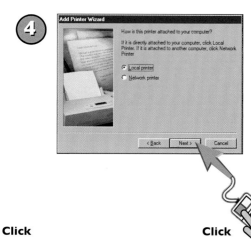

Click

Click

(✓) **Types of Printers**
Many different types of
printers are available, even
some that are designed
specifically for printing
photos (although photo
printers don't typically
work well on general tasks
such as word processing
and the like). If you already
have a color printer,
chances are that it is an
inkjet printer or a laser
printer, both of which can
deliver reasonably high-
quality pictures.

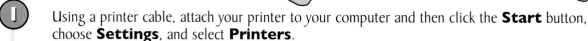

(1) Using a printer cable, attach your printer to your computer and then click the **Start** button, choose **Settings**, and select **Printers**.

(2) Double-click the **Add Printer** icon.

(3) The Add Printer Wizard starts; click **Next** to continue.

(4) If your printer is directly attached to your computer, click **Local Printer**. Otherwise, click **Network Printer**. (I've assumed you clicked **Local Printer**.)

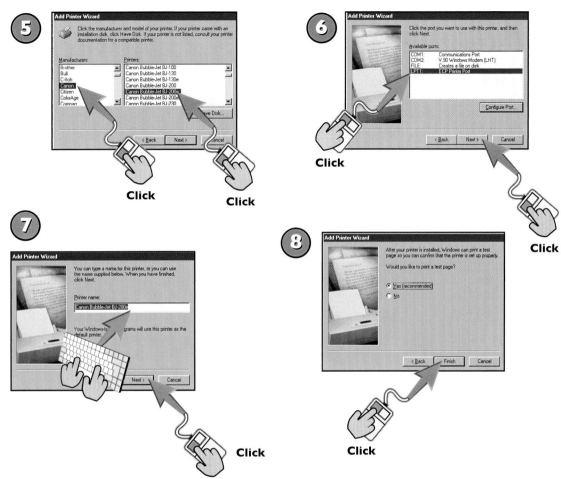

Click

Click

Click

Click

Click

Click

Click

Click

✅ **Have Disk**
If your printer came with an installation disk, click the **Have Disk** button shown in step 5, and follow the prompts.

✅ **Printer Ports**
If you're not sure which printer port to use, try **LPT1**.

✅ **Test Page Didn't Print?**
If your test page doesn't print, Windows automatically opens its Help system to enable you to troubleshoot.

5 Click the manufacturer and model of your printer, and click **Next**.

6 Select the printer port you want to use, and click **Next**.

7 If you don't like the name supplied, type a new name for your printer and click **Next**.

8 If you want to print a test page (recommended), make sure the **Yes** option button is selected, and then click **Finish**.

ArcSoft's PhotoStudio Suite, which you'll find on the CD that came with this book, is a full-featured image-editing suite. Included in the suite are PhotoBase (a program that enables you to store your photos in "albums"), PhotoFantasy (which provides sample backdrops to use with your photos), PhotoMontage (which turns your image into a mosaic of "tiles" that are actually tiny photographs), and PhotoStudio (a program that enables you to tweak your photos in any number of ways).

Task 9: Installing ArcSoft's PhotoStudio Suite on Your Machine

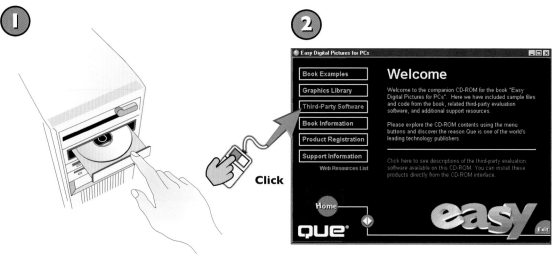

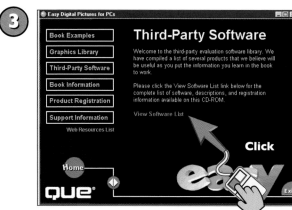

1. Insert the CD that accompanies this book into your computer's CD-ROM drive.

2. The Welcome screen appears; click **Third-Party Software**.

3. Click **View Software List**.

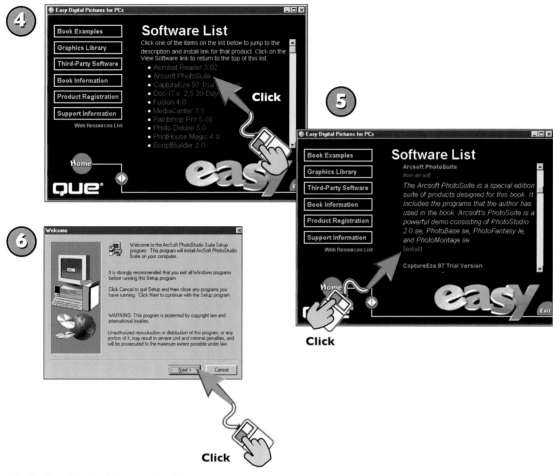

Click **ArcSoft PhotoSuite**.

Click **Install**.

Follow the directions in the Welcome screen (turn off all Windows programs), and then click **Next** to continue.

Installing ArcSoft's PhotoStudio Suite on Your Machine Continued

Start Here

7

8

Click

Click

9

Click

7   Read the software license agreement. If you agree to the conditions, choose **Yes**.

✓ **Installing Components**
I recommend that you
install all the components
of the PhotoStudio suite,
because this book covers
each one.

8   To install the program in the specified folder, click **Next**.

9   If you don't want to install some components of the suite, click to deselect them. You'll probably want to go ahead and install everything. Click **Next** to continue.

Next Step

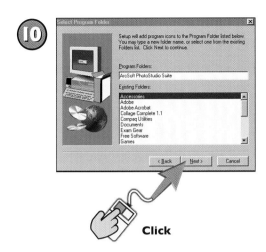

Click

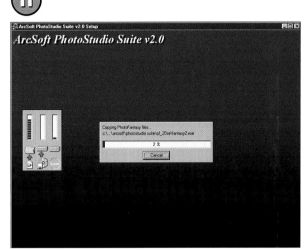

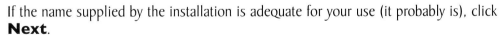

Click

If the name supplied by the installation is adequate for your use (it probably is), click **Next**.

A progress bar indicates the progress of the installation.

Click **Finish** to complete the installation.

With Corel's Print House Magic, you can easily use your images to create calendars, labels, banners, and more. This task shows you how to install Print House Magic; Part 7, "Projects," shows you how to use it!

Task 10: Installing Corel Print House Magic on Your Machine

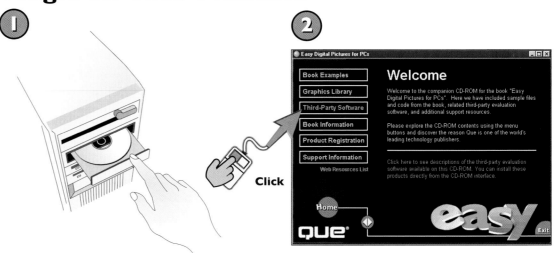

Start Here

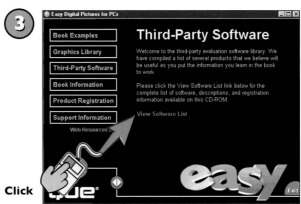

Click

✓ **Before You Install...**
Close out of any other Windows programs before you commence with the installation process.

✓ **Declining the Terms of the License Agreement**
You must click the **Accept** button after reading the license agreement to continue with the installation. If you click the **Decline** button instead of the Accept button, you are asked whether you want to terminate the installation process.

① Insert the CD that accompanies this book into your computer's CD-ROM drive.

② The Welcome screen appears; click **Third-Party Software**.

③ Click **View Software List**.

Next Step

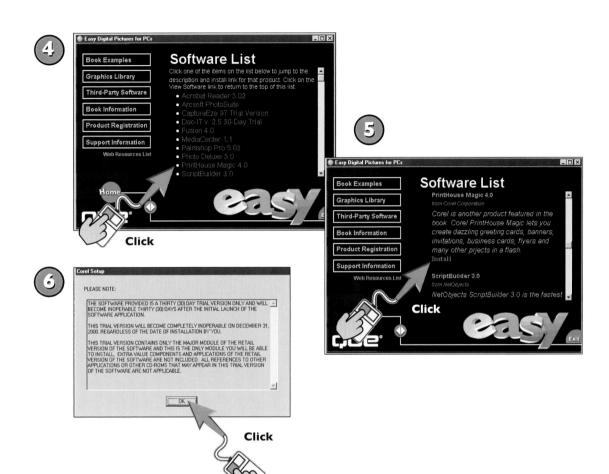

④ Click **PrintHouse Magic 4.0**.

⑤ Click **Install**.

⑥ This version of Print House Magic is a 30-day trial; click **OK** to accept this.

The Back Button
If you realize you entered incorrect information in an earlier screen, you can easily access that screen by clicking the **Back** button.

Canceling the Installation
If for some reason you need to cancel the installation, click the **Cancel** button.

Installing Corel Print House Magic on Your Machine Continued

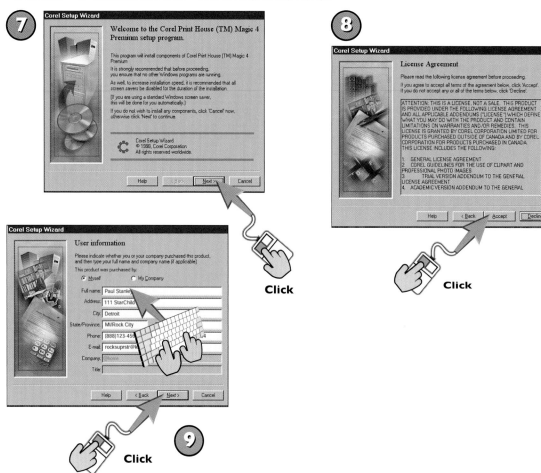

Read the information in the Welcome screen, and click **Next**.

Read the license agreement, and click **Accept**.

Fill in your user information, and click **Next**.

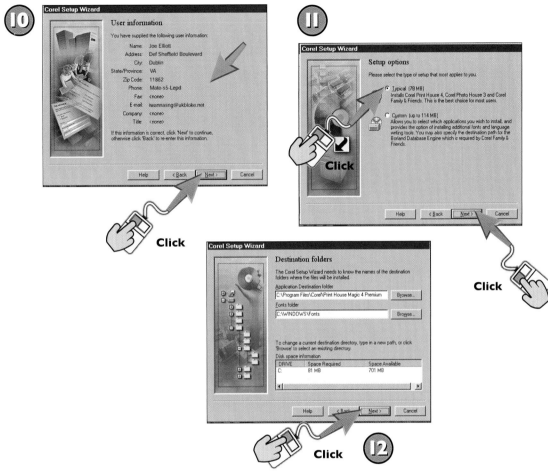

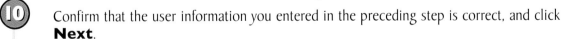

(10) Confirm that the user information you entered in the preceding step is correct, and click **Next**.

(11) Specify the type of setup you want (clicking **Typical** is your best bet), and click **Next**.

(12) Corel Print House Magic is automatically installed under the Program Files folder, and its fonts are automatically installed in the Windows\Fonts folder. Click **Next**.

✓ **The Browse Button**
If you want to install Corel Print House Magic in a folder other than the one specified in step 12, click the Browse button and select the folder you want.

Installing Corel Print House Magic on Your Machine Continued

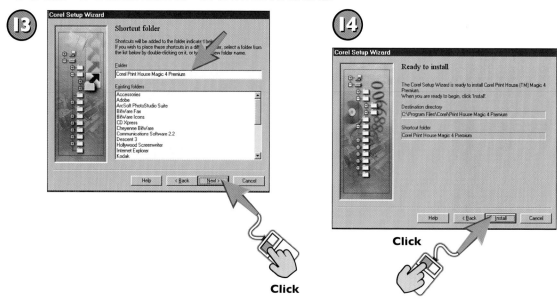

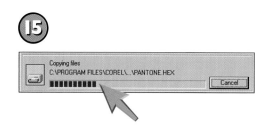

13 A shortcut to Print House Magic will be installed in the folder specified. If you want the shortcut installed in another folder, click it. Either way, click **Next**.

14 Click **Install**.

15 A progress bar indicates the progress of your installation; it might take a moment or two to complete.

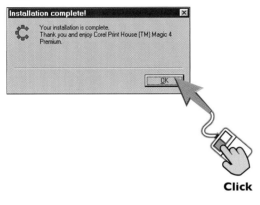

Click

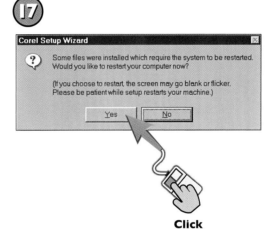

Click

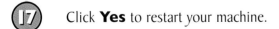
A message box indicates that your installation is complete; click **OK**.

Click **Yes** to restart your machine.

End
Task

✓ Close Other Programs!
If you didn't close out of all other programs before you began the installation process, be sure to do so before you click the Yes option button in step 17.

Task 11: Installing NetObjects Fusion

NetObjects Fusion is a program that makes it easy to build Web pages of your own.

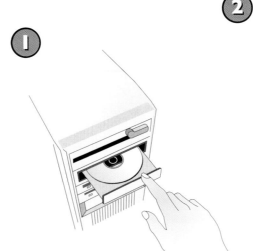

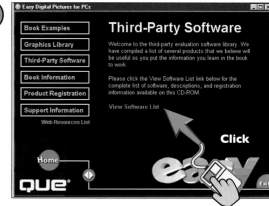

Click

Click

✅ **Before You Install...**
Close out of any other Windows programs before you commence with the installation process.

✅ **The Back Button**
If you realize you entered incorrect information in an earlier screen, you can easily access that screen by clicking the **Back** button.

① Insert the CD that accompanies this book into your computer's CD drive.

② The Welcome screen appears; click **Third-Party Software**.

③ Click **View Software List**.

Next Step

Click **Fusion 4.0**.

Click **Install**.

Click the **Setup** button to unzip the setup files and begin the installation.

✅ Canceling the Installation
If for some reason you need to cancel the installation, click the **Cancel** button.

✅ Declining the Terms of the License Agreement
You must click the **Yes** button after reading the license agreement to continue with the installation. If you click the **No** button instead, you are asked whether you want to terminate the installation process.

Installing NetObjects Fusion Continued

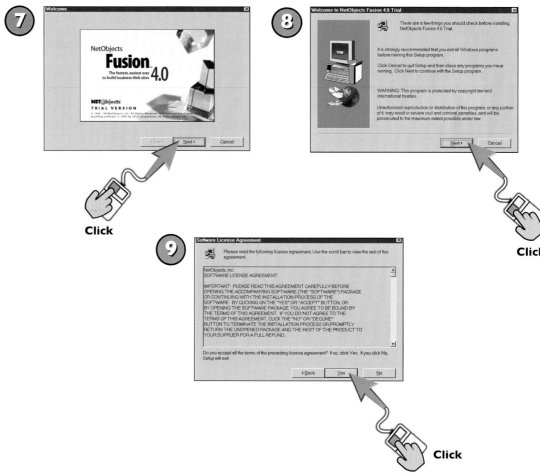

⑦ Click **Next** to continue.

⑧ Read the information in the dialog box, and click **Next**.

⑨ Read the license agreement, and click **Yes**.

Next
Step

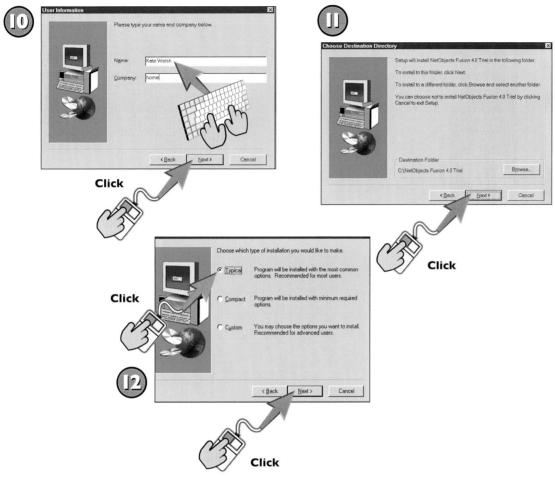

Click

Click

Click

Click

10 Type your name and the company you work for. If this is for home use, simply type **Home**. Click **Next**.

11 NetObjects Fusion is automatically installed under the Program Files folder. Click **Next**.

12 Specify whether you want a typical, compact, or custom installation (I'm going with typical), and click **Next**.

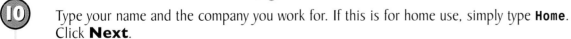

✅ **The Browse Button**
If you want to install NetObjects Fusion in a folder other than the one specified in step 11, click the **Browse** button and select the folder you want.

Installing NetObjects Fusion Continued

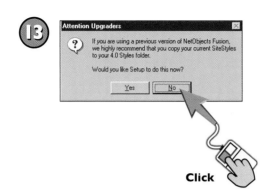

Attention Upgraders

If you are using a previous version of NetObjects Fusion, we highly recommend that you copy your current SiteStyles to your 4.0 Styles folder.

Would you like Setup to do this now?

Yes   No

Click

Now Copying Program Files...
c:\netobjects fusion 4.0 trial\netobjects system\nfxcomponentutil.jar

31 %

Cancel

Display ReadMe?

Would you like to view the Readme.htm file now?

Yes   No

Click

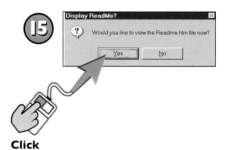

Click **No** if no previous versions of Fusion are installed on your computer.

A progress bar indicates the progress of your installation.

You are prompted to view the Readme.htm file; click **Yes**.

Next Step

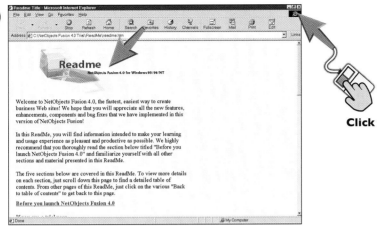

Click

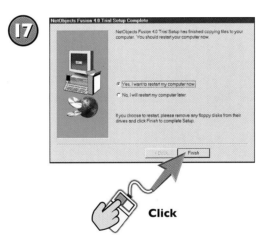

Click

16 The Readme.htm file opens in a browser window. Read the file, and close the browser window by clicking the **Close (X)** button.

17 Click **Finish** to restart your computer and complete the setup.

PART 2

Obtaining Images

You can obtain images to work with on your computer by using a digital camera, a scanner, a PhotoCD, and more. This part covers the ways in which you acquire the images you want to manipulate.

Tasks

Task 1: Using a Digital Camera

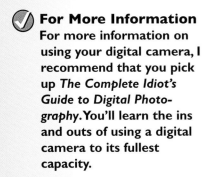

Different cameras offer different features; this task is designed to introduce those features, using Kodak's **DC240** as a model (note: the precise features and operations of your camera may differ).

✓ **For More Information**
For more information on using your digital camera, I recommend that you pick up *The Complete Idiot's Guide to Digital Photography.* You'll learn the ins and outs of using a digital camera to its fullest capacity.

✓ **Tripod**
If you want to use a tripod, simply screw it into the threaded hole in the bottom of the camera.

✓ **Camera Setup**
Set the dial on the back of the camera to **Camera Setup** to set the current date (displayed on pictures), the video output mode, power-saving features, auto flash, the white balance, and more.

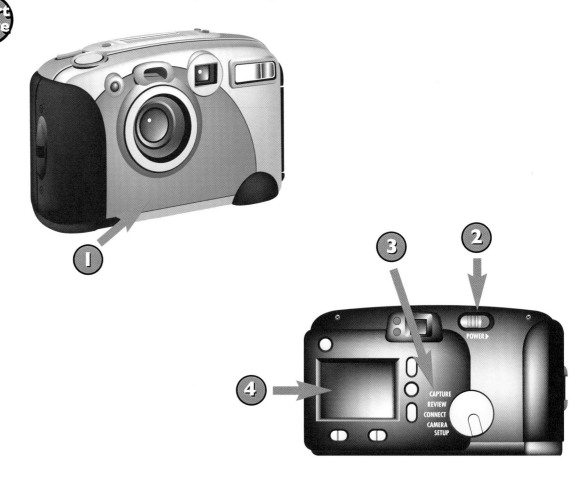

① The front of the DC240 is shown here.

② On the back of the camera, flip the power switch.

③ Make sure the dial is set to **Capture**.

④ Use either the LCD screen or the view window to frame your subject.

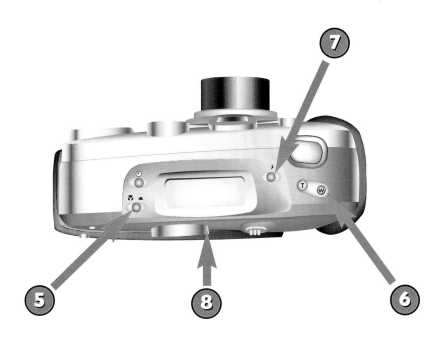

Self Timer

Press the button that is marked with a clock on the top of the camera to use the self timer.

Adjusting the Brightness

The Kodak DC240 has a small dial on the bottom of the camera that enables you to adjust the brightness of the image. Because digital cameras typically require more light than film-based ones, don't be surprised to find yourself using the brightest setting!

Reviewing Your Images

To review your images, set the dial on the back of the camera to Review, press the Menu button to the top left of the LCD screen, and use the buttons surrounding the LCD screen to zoom in on, delete, change the print order of, lock in, or change the names of images, or to generate a slideshow to display on the LCD screen.

5 Press the button marked by images of a mountain (for when your subject is far away) and a flower (for close-ups) to set the focus range.

6 Press **T** or **W** to specify whether the lens acts like a telephoto lens or a wide-angle lens.

7 Press the button marked by a lightning rod to enable or disable the flash.

8 The screen on top of the camera displays the settings. When you're satisfied with them and with the image in your viewfinder/LCD screen, press the shutter button.

End Task

Task 2: Transferring Files from Your Camera to Your Hard Drive

To view and manipulate your images using your computer, you must first download them from your camera to your machine. This task shows you how using the Kodak DC240 and the Kodak Picture Easy software as a model (your camera and software may differ; check your camera's manual for more information).

✅ **Install Your Camera's Software**

You must install your camera's acquisition software on your computer before you can perform this task. Because the installation process differs depending on the type of camera you have, I do not cover that installation process here. Refer to your camera's documentation for details.

✅ **Picture Cards**

Some cameras use removable picture cards to store the images you take with your camera; using a special device, you can transfer images directly from the disk after you've removed it from the camera.

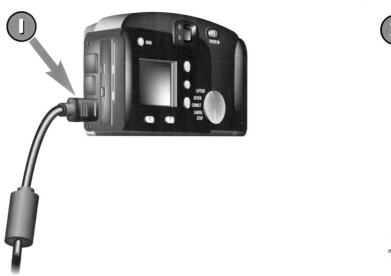

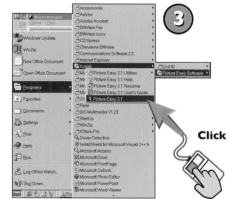

Click

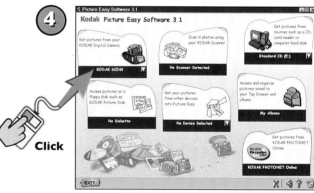

Click

 Connect one end of the cable that came with your camera into the correct slot in the camera body. (This slot in the Kodak DC240 is marked by two opposite-facing arrows.)

 Connect the other end of the cable into your computer's serial port.

 Start your camera's acquisition software (mine's Kodak Picture Easy). If you're not sure what type of software you use, check your camera's documentation.

 Select **Get Pictures from Your KODAK Digital Camera** (you may need to select the correct model from the drop-down list).

Next Step

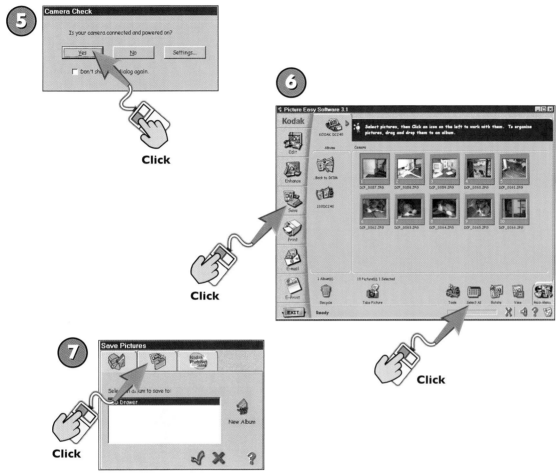

Click

Click

Click

Click

Click

✔ **See Only One Image?**
If after you download images from your camera only one image appears, try double-clicking its lower-left corner to display the rest.

✔ **Pick and Choose**
If you want to save only selected images, do not click the Select All button. Instead, press and hold the **Ctrl** key and click the thumbnails of the images you want to save.

✔ **Renaming Images**
It's hard to remember which images are which when they have names like DCP_0057.jpg. I recommend renaming your images so that they have more descriptive names, such as puppy.jpg or mom.jpg. To do so, open **Windows Explorer**, navigate to the folder where the images reside, select the image that you want to rename, open the **File** menu, choose **Rename**, and type the new name (don't forget the extension!).

5 When asked if your camera is connected and powered on, click **Yes**.

6 Any pictures currently being stored on your camera's hard drive are downloaded to your computer. Click the **Select All** button, and then click **Save**.

7 Click the middle tab, specify the folder where you want the images to be saved, and click **Save**. The images are saved to your hard drive.

End Task

Task 3: Scanning Your Photo Prints

No doubt you took photographs with a traditional film-based camera before you went digital. Fear not—that shoebox full of prints won't go to waste! You can use a scanner to convert your print photos to digital images.

✓ Flatbed Versus Hand-Held

Flatbed scanners resemble small copy machines; you lay the photo face down on the glass, close the lid, and let 'er rip. (Note: Certain flatbed scanners let you scan slides. Check your scanner's documentation to see if it offers this feature.) Hand-held scanners, which are covered here, roll over the top of a face-up image to gather digital information.

✓ Installing Scanner Software

Make sure you've installed your scanner's software before you proceed with this task; refer to your scanner's documentation if you need help.

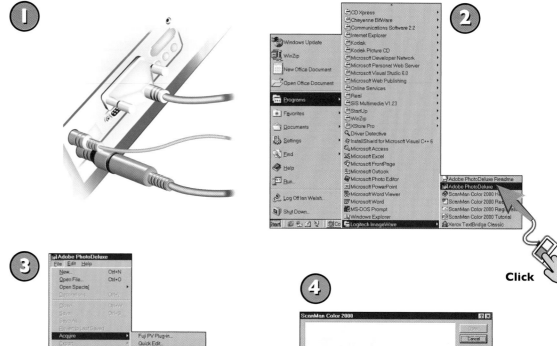

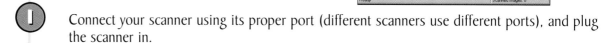

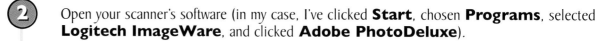

① Connect your scanner using its proper port (different scanners use different ports), and plug the scanner in.

② Open your scanner's software (in my case, I've clicked **Start**, chosen **Programs**, selected **Logitech ImageWare**, and clicked **Adobe PhotoDeluxe**).

③ PhotoDeluxe opens; open the **File** menu, choose **Acquire**, and select your scanner from the list (in this example, **ScanMan Color 2000**).

④ The **ScanMan Color 2000** window opens, giving you various options. Specify the document type and the scan direction.

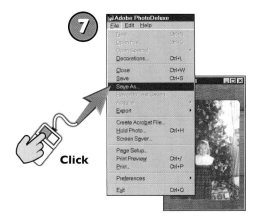

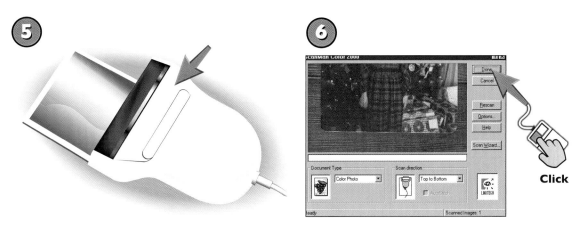

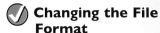

Changing the File Format

When you save your image in PhotoDeluxe via the Save As command, you can use only the **PDD** file format. If you want to save to a different format, such as JPEG (recommended for photos) or TIFF, you must open the **File** menu, choose **Export**, and select **File Formats**. In the Export dialog box, locate the folder where you want to store the image, provide a descriptive name, and select a file format from the **Save As** drop-down list. You have several options, including **BMP, TIF, PCX, GIF, TGA**, and **JPEG**. For more information about each of these options, see the glossary.

Click

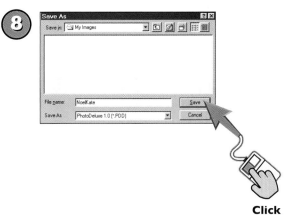

Click

Click

Cropping Out the Background

You might have noticed that the image I scanned shows the table it was sitting on in the background. You'll learn how to crop such unsightly things from your images in the next part.

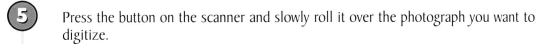

(5) Press the button on the scanner and slowly roll it over the photograph you want to digitize.

(6) The image appears onscreen as it is scanned. When the entire image has been scanned, click the button on the scanner, and then click the **Done** button onscreen.

(7) The image appears on your desktop. To rename and save it, open the **File** menu and choose **Save As**.

(8) Locate the folder where you want to store the image, type a descriptive name in the **File Name** field, and click **Save**.

Task 4: Acquiring Images from Kodak Picture CDs

With a PhotoCD, you need not purchase a digital camera to obtain digital images. Instead, you simply order a PhotoCD of your prints when you have your film developed. You can use your PhotoCD software to view, modify, print, or email images and more. This task shows you how to export images from your PhotoCD to your hard drive for later use.

✔ Auto Launch Not Working?

Depending on your computer's configuration, the Kodak Picture CD's Auto Launch feature (which starts the installation software automatically) might not work. If nothing happens the first time you put the CD in the CD-ROM drive, open Windows Explorer (click **Start**, choose **Programs**, and select **Windows Explorer**), click the icon for your CD-ROM drive, and then double-click the file named **Launch.exe**.

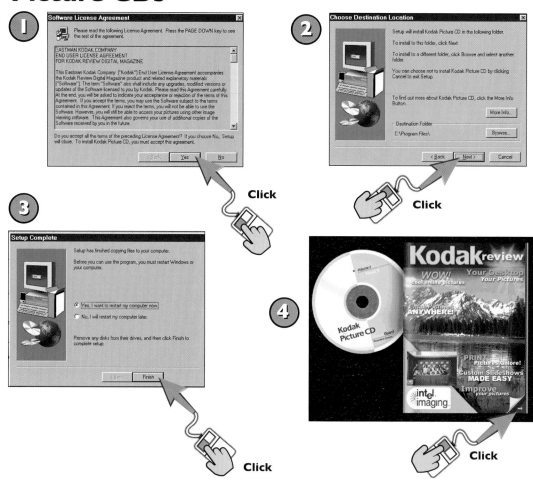

Start Here

① **Click**

② **Click**

③ **Click**

④ **Click**

① Insert the PhotoCD in your computer's CD-ROM drive; the Kodak Picture CD's installation software launches automatically. Read the license agreement, and click **Yes**.

② Kodak's Picture CD program is installed in the **Program Files** file by default, which is probably where you want it. Click **Next** to continue.

③ Click the **Yes** option button to restart your computer (close all other programs and remove the PhotoCD from the disk drive first), and then click **Finish**.

④ Re-insert the PhotoCD; its software launches automatically. After the pictures are loaded and you view a short movie, click the right-arrow button.

Next Step

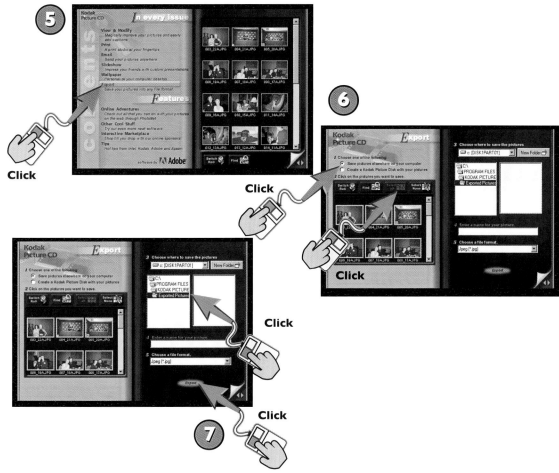

Switching Rolls
PhotoCDs can store multiple rolls of film that were developed at the same time. To view images from another roll of film, click **Switch Roll** and select the roll you want from the list that appears.

Naming the Files
If you are exporting only a single image to your hard drive, PhotoCD enables you to change the image's filename. This enables you to give your images descriptive names, which will help you keep them sorted in the future.

File Formats
You can save your images in a variety of file formats. I recommend using the JPEG format for your digital images.

5 Click the **Export** option.

6 Click the **Save Pictures Elsewhere on Your Computer** option button, and click **Select All**.

7 Specify the folder on your hard drive where you want to save your pictures (you can even create a new folder if you want), change the file format if desired, and click **Export**.

Task 5: Obtaining Images from Kodak's PhotoNet Web Site

Suppose you just shot a roll of film on your regular camera, and you know there are images on there that you'll want in digital form. Fortunately, you can have the images on that roll of film posted on Kodak's own Web site. All you need to do is check the appropriate box on the envelope when you drop off your film. After your film is developed, you'll be able to jump online and download your images.

✓ **You Must Be Online**
You must be connected to the Internet when performing this task.

✓ **Already Have an Account?**
If you already have an account, simply type your email address and password in the screen shown in step 3.

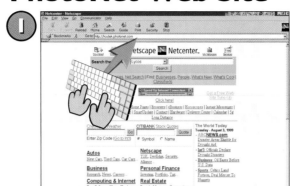
Click

Click

Click

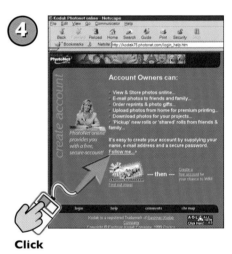
Click

1 With your Web browser open, type **http://kodak.photonet.com** in the Address bar.

2 An alert box might appear to notify you that the site you've requested is secure. If you don't want to be notified again, uncheck **Show This Alert Next Time**. Click **Continue**.

3 If this is the first time you've used Kodak's PhotoNet site, you'll need to create an account. To do so, click the **Create Your Free Account** link.

4 Click the **Follow Me** link.

Next Step

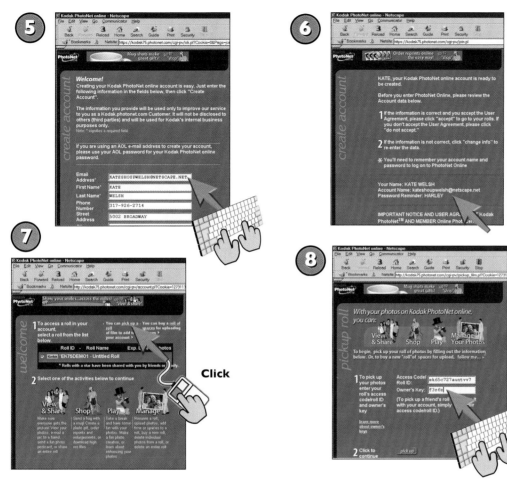

5 Enter the requested information (name, address, phone number, and a password), and click **Create Account**.

6 Verify that the information you entered is correct, read the license agreement (you'll need to scroll down), and click **Accept**.

7 Click the **Pick Up a Roll** link.

8 Enter the access code and owner's key (refer to the claim card that came with your prints) and click **Pick Up**.

✓ **Change Info**
If, when you're verifying your information in step 6, you discover that it is incorrect, you can correct it by clicking the **Change Info** button at the bottom of the page.

✓ **The Claim Card**
When you pick up your prints, you'll find a claim card in the same envelope. This claim card contains your owner key and the access code you need to pick up your digital images online.

Obtaining Images from Kodak's PhotoNet Web Site Continued

✓ **Sharing the Roll**

If you want your friends and family to be able to view your roll of pictures on the PhotoNet Web site, scroll down to the bottom of the page shown in step 9, enter the recipient's email address (to share the roll with multiple recipients, separate each address with a comma), type a brief message, and click **Share Roll**. Kodak sends a message telling the recipient how to use the Web site to access the photos!

✓ **Emailing Photos**

To email photos directly from the Web site, click the **[E-mail Photos]** link at the top of the page shown in step 9, and click the check boxes under the images you want to email to select them. Then, scroll to the bottom of the page, enter the recipient's email address, type a subject and a brief message, and click **Preview E-mail**. You see a preview of the message; click **Send E-mail** to send it.

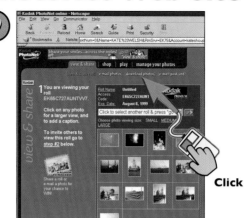

Click

Click

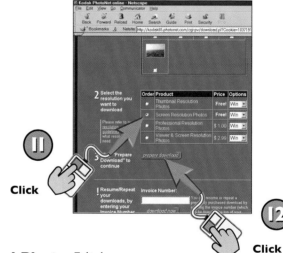

Click

Click

Click

 Click the **[Download Photos]** link.

 Click the **All Photos** check box if you want to download all the images to your hard drive. Otherwise, click the check boxes under the individual images that you want.

 Scroll down the page, and select the resolution you want (click the **Resolution Guidelines** link if you're not sure what you want).

Click **Prepare Download**.

Next Step

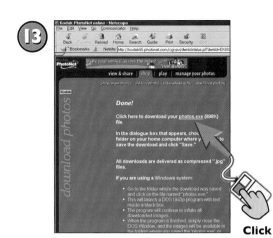

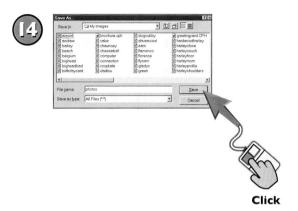

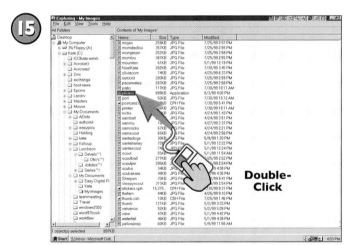

Click

Click

Double-Click

Sending a Digital Postcard

If you want to send a digital postcard of one of your images, click the **[E-mail Postcard]** link at the top of the page shown in step 9, and click the option button under the image you want to send. Then, scroll to the bottom of the page, type a brief message, enter the recipient's email address (to email the postcard to multiple recipients, separate each address with a comma), and click **Preview Postcard.** You see a preview of the postcard; click **Send Postcard** to send it.

Closing Your Browser

Click the **Close (X)** button in the upper-right corner of your browser window to close it.

Closing the DOS Window

Click the **Close (X)** button in the upper-right corner of the DOS window to close it.

13 Click the **photos.exe** link.

14 Find the folder on your hard drive where you want to store the pictures, and click **Save**.

15 In Windows Explorer, navigate to the folder where you saved your images in the last step, and double-click the **photos.exe** file.

16 A DOS UnZip program is launched, inflating (that is, decompressing) the images and placing them in the folder.

Task 6: Obtaining Images Via Email

If someone sends you an image attached to an email message, you can easily save it to your hard drive. This task shows you how to do so using Microsoft Outlook; if you use a different email program, search the help files for information about saving attachments.

Double-Click

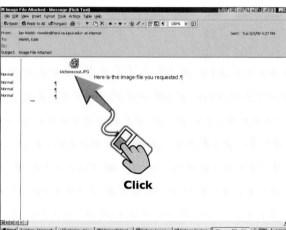

Click

Double-click the message containing the image you want to save.

The image opens. Click the attachment to select it.

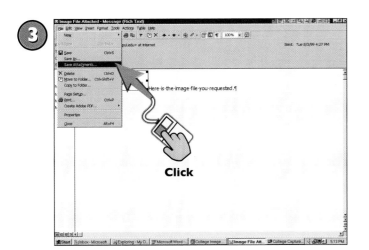

Click

Click

3 Open the **File** menu and choose **Save Attachments**.

4 Find the folder on your hard drive where you want to store the pictures, and click **Save**.

Task 7: Using the Image Bank on the CD-ROM

This book's companion CD contains an image bank filled with all sorts of stock images that you can use—animals, people, places, and more. This task shows you how to use the image bank.

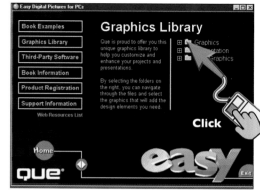

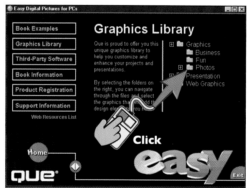

✓ Web Graphics
For you Webophiles out there, the Web Graphics folder offers numerous banners, buttons, tiles, and textures that you can use for your Web pages.

✓ Presentation Backgrounds
Click the Presentation folder to access some interesting images that can serve as backgrounds to your photographs, Web pages, and so on.

(1) After you've inserted this book's companion CD into your CD-ROM drive, click **Graphics Library**.

(2) You have three options: Graphics, Presentation, and Web Graphics. Click the **Graphics** folder.

(3) You'll find stock photos under the Business, Fun, and Photos folders; for now, click **Photos**.

(4) You have three options under the Photos folder: Animals, Everyday, and People. Click any of these subfolders (I've chosen **Animals**).

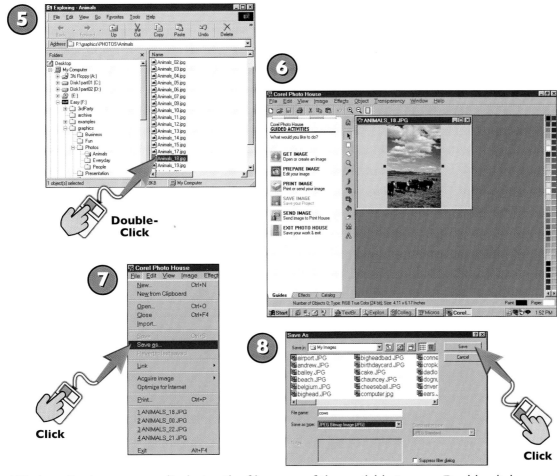

Double-Click

Click

Click

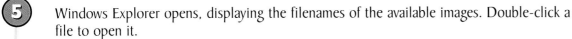

⑤ Windows Explorer opens, displaying the filenames of the available images. Double-click a file to open it.

⑥ The image opens.

⑦ To save the image to your hard drive, open the **File** menu and choose **Save As**.

⑧ Find the spot on your hard drive where you want to save the file, name the file, and select a file type from the **Save as Type** drop-down list. Click **Save**.

File Types
Notice that the Save as File Type drop-down list offers several options, including **BMP, TIF, PCX, GIF, TGA,** and **JPEG.** For more information about these options, see the glossary.

End Task

PART 3

PhotoStudio Basics

Before you start using PhotoStudio for the really fun stuff, like putting your dog's head on your kid's body and applying the Oil Painting filter to your family reunion pictures, you'll want to learn some PhotoStudio basics. That way, if you dream up a project that's not covered in this book, you'll have the tools you need to figure out how to make it work.

Tasks

Task 1: Starting PhotoStudio

First, the most basic of the basics: starting PhotoStudio.

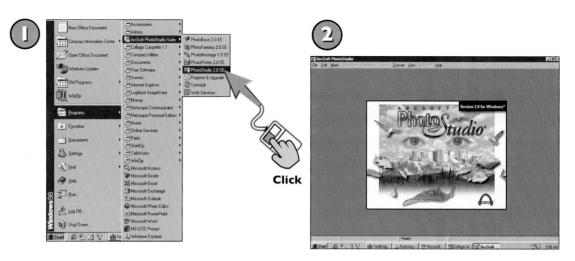

Click

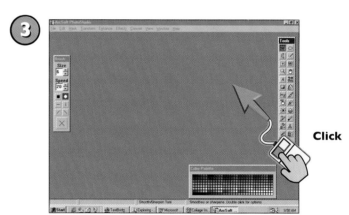

Click

① Click the **Start** button, choose **Programs**, select **ArcSoft PhotoStudio Suite**, and click **PhotoStudio 2.0 SE**.

② PhotoStudio opens.

③ Click anywhere on the screen to eliminate the PhotoStudio graphic and view the desktop.

Task 2: Opening Images in PhotoStudio

Start Here

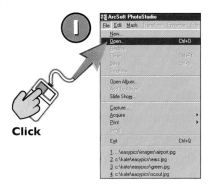

Click

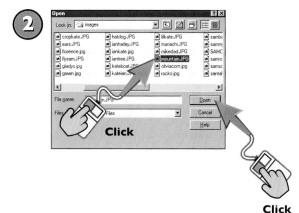

Click

Click

Before you can manipulate images in PhotoStudio, you must first learn how to open them. This task shows you how.

1 Open the **File** menu and choose **Open**.

2 Navigate to the folder containing the image you want to open, find the image, click to select it, and then click the **Open** button.

3 The image file opens on the desktop.

✓ **Keyboard Shortcut**
To avoid using the menus, simply press **Ctrl+O**.

✓ **Using an Album**
In addition to being able to retrieve pictures you've stored in a folder on your hard drive, you can also retrieve pictures from your photo album (see **Part 6,** "Storing Digital Images Using PhotoStudio's Album Feature," for more information about creating photo albums). To do so, open the **File** menu, choose **Open Album,** select the album that contains the photo you want to use, and then double-click the picture itself.

End Task

Task 3: Manipulating the PhotoStudio Desktop

You can easily adjust the PhotoStudio desktop to your liking. For example, you can hide the **Brush, Tools,** and **Color** palettes; you can also move, tile, and cascade open image files. This is handy if you're working with multiple files and the desktop becomes too crowded.

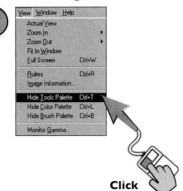

Click

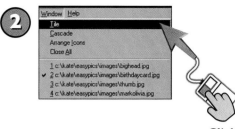

Click

Click & Drag

Restoring Palettes
To restore the Brush, Tools, or Color palette to view, open the **View** menu and choose **Show Tools Palette, Show Brush Palette,** or **Show Color Palette.**

1 Open the **View** menu and choose **Hide Tools Palette, Hide Brush Palette,** or **Hide Color Palette**.

2 To tile the open windows, making them easier to view, open the **Window** menu and choose **Tile**.

3 The images are tiled. To move an image, click its title bar, hold down the mouse button, and drag the image window into place.

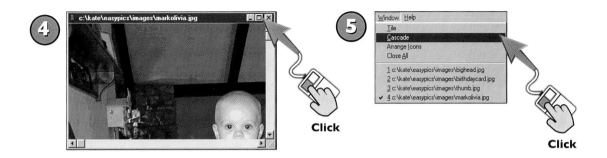

Click

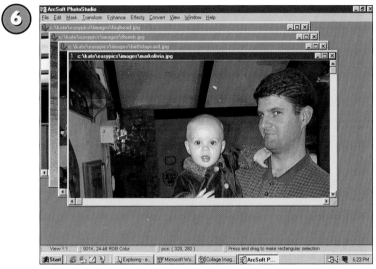

Click

④ To view an image full-size, click the **Maximize** button in the upper-right corner of the image window.

⑤ The image is maximized. To cascade the open images on the desktop, open the **Window** menu and choose **Cascade**.

⑥ The images are cascaded on the desktop.

Task 4: Acquiring Images from Your Digital Camera in PhotoStudio

Let's face it, importing images from your camera, saving them to your hard drive, and then opening PhotoStudio and using the File, Open command to open the image you just imported can be time consuming. Fortunately, PhotoStudio provides a way for you to acquire images from your camera directly from the PhotoStudio desktop. You still use your camera's acquisition software, but don't have to take all those extra steps!

✓ **Camera Setup**
Every digital camera setup is different; use the documentation that came with your camera to connect it to your computer.

✓ **Software**
The acquisition software that came with your camera must be installed for you to be able to acquire images from your camera—even if you're using PhotoStudio to do it!

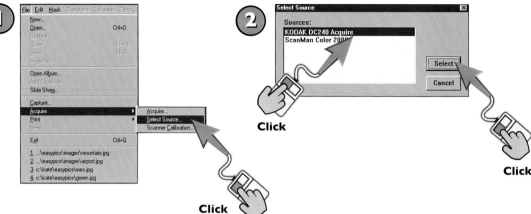

Click

Click

Click

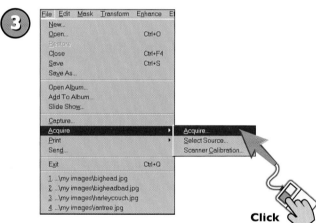

Click

① Open the **File** menu, choose **Acquire**, and click **Select Source**.

② Click the source (in this example, **KODAK DC240 Acquire**), and click **Select**.

③ Again, open the **File** menu and choose **Acquire**, but this time select the **Acquire** submenu.

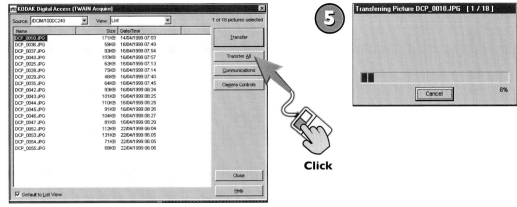

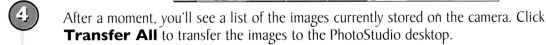

(4) After a moment, you'll see a list of the images currently stored on the camera. Click **Transfer All** to transfer the images to the PhotoStudio desktop.

(5) A progress bar keeps you apprised of the progress of the transfer (the transfer can take awhile).

(6) The images are transferred from the camera to the PhotoStudio desktop.

 Different Screen?
Don't be surprised if the screens you see from step 4 on are different from the ones shown here; every camera comes with different software. If necessary, use your camera's documentation as a guide to complete this task.

End Task

Task 5: Acquiring Images from a Scanner in PhotoStudio

Scanning photographs directly into PhotoStudio is similar to importing images from your camera. Using PhotoStudio's Acquire command, you can scan an image directly onto the PhotoStudio desktop. You still use your scanner's acquisition software to do it, but you don't have to open that program separately.

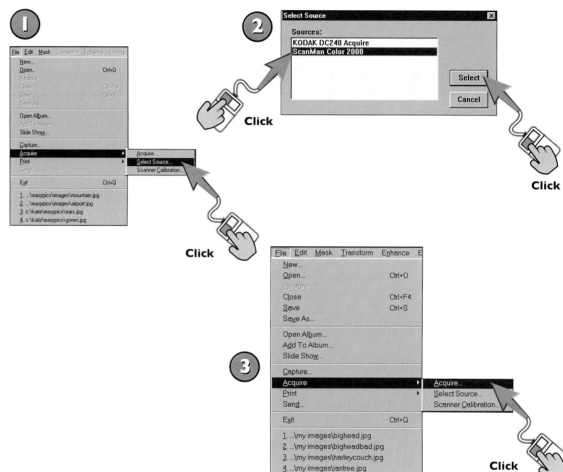

Start Here

Click

Click

Click

Click

✓ **Scanner Setup**
Every scanner setup is different; use the documentation that came with your scanner to connect it to your computer.

✓ **Hand-Held Scanner**
This task covers the use of a hand-held scanner. If you are using a flatbed scanner, the steps you must take will be similar to the ones here, except that you won't need to actually roll the scanner across the photograph.

1 Open the **File** menu, choose **Acquire**, and click **Select Source**.

2 Click the source (in this example, **ScanMan Color 2000**), and click **Select**.

3 Again, open the **File** menu and choose **Acquire**, but this time select the **Acquire** submenu.

Next Step

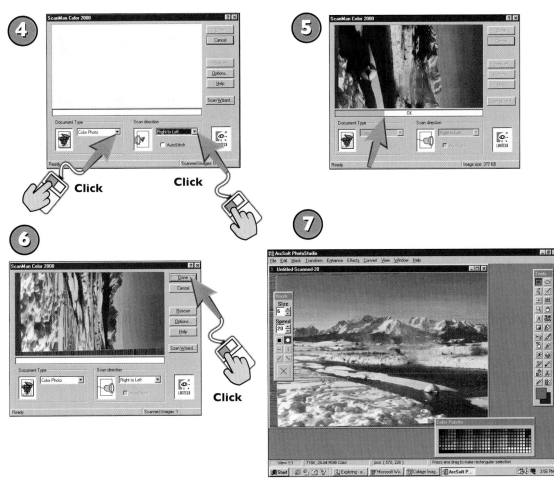

4 Click Click

5

6 Click

7

Software
The acquisition software that came with your scanner must be installed for you to be able to acquire images from your scanner—even if you're using PhotoStudio to do it!

Different Screen?
Don't be surprised if the screens you see from step 4 on are different from the ones shown here; every scanner comes with different software. If necessary, use your scanner's documentation as a guide to complete this task.

Cropping
You'll probably find that your scanned images need to be cropped, because scanners often scan the surface underneath the photo in addition to the photo itself (in this case, you get a good look at the grain on my dining room table). To crop the image, see Task 2, "Cropping Images," of Part 4, "Touching Up Your Images with PhotoStudio."

4 My scanner software asks that I specify the document type (color photo) and scan direction (right to left).

5 Roll the hand-held scanner over the photograph to scan it (you might have to press a button on the scanner first). View the progress of the scan on your screen.

6 When you're finished with the scan (you might need to press a button on the scanner to indicate that you're finished), click the **Done** button.

7 The scanned image appears on the PhotoStudio desktop.

Task 6: Saving Images

After you've acquired images from a scanner or camera, you'll need to save them to your hard drive. Additionally, you'll need to save any image files you edit using PhotoStudio if you want your changes to remain intact. This task shows you how.

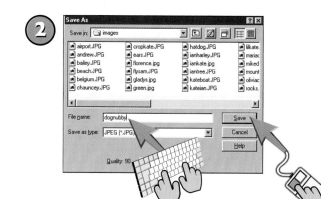

Click

Click

✓ **The Quality Slider**

If you are more concerned about the size of the file than its image quality, use the **Quality** slider at the bottom of the Save As dialog box to compress the file, making it easier to store and to transport. The lower the Quality setting, the more the file is compressed.

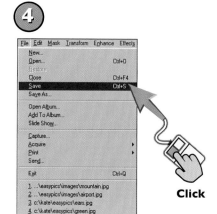

Click

✓ **File Types**

Notice that the Save as File Type drop-down list offers several options, including BMP, TIF, PCX, GIF, TGA, and JPEG. For more information about each of these options, see the glossary.

(1) To save a newly acquired image, begin by clicking the image to select it. Then open the **File** menu and choose **Save As**.

(2) Specify the spot on your hard drive where you want the image to be stored, name it, select a file type, and click **Save**.

(3) The image is saved with the name you specified.

(4) After you edit the image, save changes to it by opening the **File** menu and choosing **Save**.

End Task

Task 7: Flipping Images Vertically or Horizontally

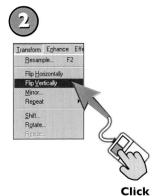

Click

Sometimes, images that you've scanned or acquired from your digital camera end up upside down or backwards on the desktop. This task shows you how to flip your images.

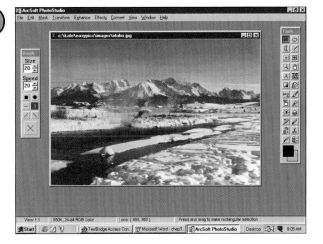

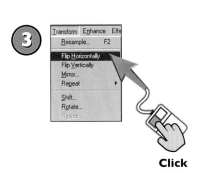

Click

① Open the image that needs to be flipped.

② Because this image is upside-down, open the **Transform** menu and choose **Flip Vertically**.

③ The image is flipped. To rotate the image left-to-right, open the **Transform** menu and choose **Flip Horizontally**.

④ The image is reversed.

 Rotating Images
To rotate a horizontal image into a vertical one (or vice versa), follow the steps in Task 9, "Rotating Images."

Task 8: Adjusting Width, Height, and Resolution

When you adjust an image's width, height, or resolution, this is called *resampling*. This is different from adjusting the width or height of the window that contains the image, as you did in the last step; resampling changes the actual height and width (and, if you so choose, resolution) information in the image file itself.

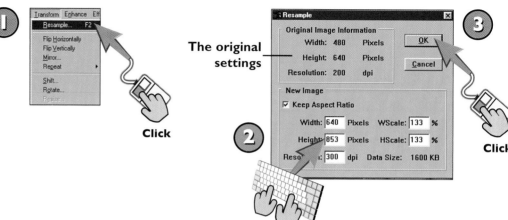

The original settings

Click

Click

(✓) **Resolution**
Changing an image's resolution (its pixel density) might or might not affect the appearance of that image on the screen, although it's a general rule of thumb that higher-resolution images have greater density and better appearance.

(✓) **WScale and HScale**
Adjusting the WScale and HScale settings sets a new width or height (respectively) for the image based on percentage of the original width or height.

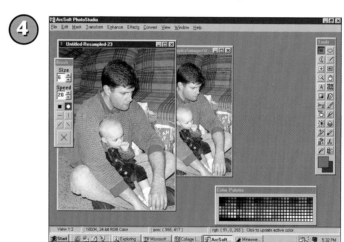

① With the image you want to resample open on the desktop, open the **Transform** menu and choose **Resample**.

② With **Keep Aspect Ratio** checked, type a new height or width. Notice that the **Width**, **Height**, **WScale**, and **HScale** values are all changed to reflect your entry.

③ If you want to change the resolution, type the new value in the **Resolution** field, and click **OK**.

④ A resampled copy of the image is generated.

Task 9: Rotating Images

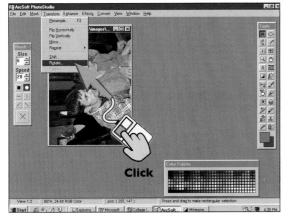

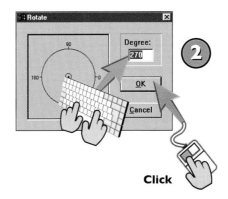

When you acquire images from your camera, you might find that some images that should be vertical appear horizontal, and vice versa. Fortunately, PhotoStudio makes this easy to correct.

1 With the image that needs to be rotated on the desktop, open the **Transform** menu and choose **Rotate**.

2 In the Rotate dialog box, specify the degree by which the image should be rotated. In this case, I've changed the entry in the **Degree** field from **0** to **270**.

3 The image is rotated, but the window needs to be resized.

4 Hover your pointer over the window's right border (the pointer becomes a two-headed arrow), click, and drag. Repeat on the bottom border.

If you want to zoom in on part of your image to get a better look, you can use either the **View** menu or the **Tools** palette to do it. This task shows you how.

Task 10: Using Zoom

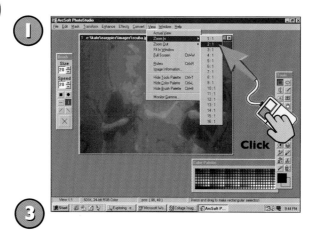

Click

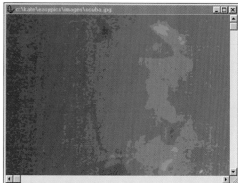

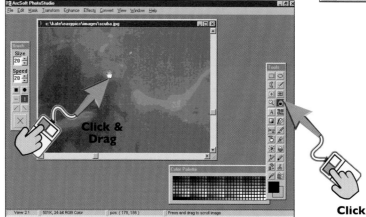

Click & Drag

Click

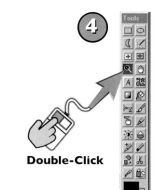

Double-Click

Open the **View** menu, choose **Zoom In**, and select the zoom ratio that suits your needs.

② Although the image itself is not in fact larger, you see a portion of it in detail view, making it appear so.

 Scrollbars
If you're not comfortable using the Grabber tool, try using the scrollbars to navigate within a zoomed image.

③ Click the **Grabber** tool. When you hover over the image, the pointer changes to a hand; click and drag to view a different portion of the image.

④ Double-click the **Zoom** tool in the Tools palette to return the image to the actual (non-zoomed) view.

Next Step

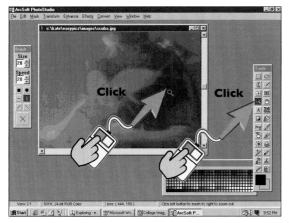

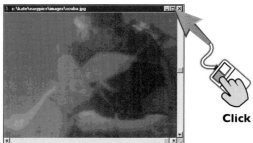

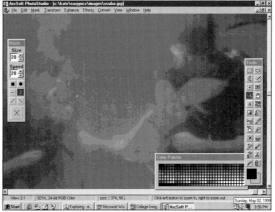

To zoom a specific portion of the image, click the **Zoom** tool, and then click the portion of the image you want to zoom.

To maximize your window so you can view more of a zoomed image, click the **Maximize** button in the top-right corner of the window.

The window is maximized.

✓ **Zooming Out**
Although it's rarely useful, you can zoom out on your image, as well—but doing this makes it so small it's hard to see much at all.

Task 11: Using Selection Tools

PhotoStudio's selection tools enable you to select *masks*, which are areas of your image that you want to edit. You'll use masks anytime you want to crop an image, apply a filter, or copy and paste portions of an image. You can use different selection tools to select different types of masks.

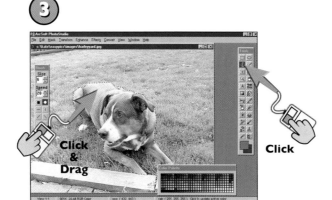

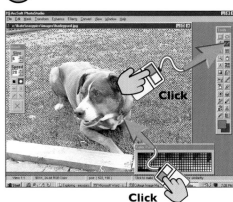

✅ **Circles and Squares**
To select a perfect square or circle, double-click the **Rectangle Select** or **Ellipse Select** tool, respectively. Then, in the dialog box that opens, click the **Square** or **Circle** check box (other options enable you to specify that the square or circle be drawn from the center and that the square or circle be of a fixed size that you specify), and click **OK**.

1. Click the **Rectangle Select** tool. Then click and drag over the part of the image you want to select.

2. Click the **Ellipse Select** tool. Then click and drag over the part of the image you want to select.

3. Click the **Freehand Select** tool. Then, click and drag to trace the portion of the image you want to select. When you're finished, double-click to set the mask.

4. Click the **Magic Wand** tool, and then click a spot in the image to select all portions of the image that are that color.

Next Step

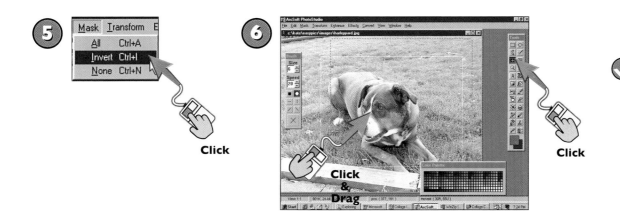

Click

Click

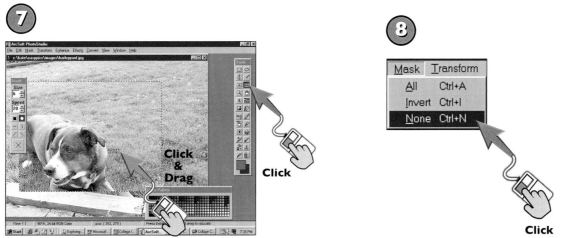

Click & Drag

Click

Click

Magic Wand
If you used the **Magic Wand** tool to select all portions of the image that are a certain color, but only some portions ended up getting selected, try double-clicking the **Magic Wand** tool in the toolbar and unchecking the **Contiguous Area Only** check box in the dialog box that appears. Conversely, suppose you want to select the sky but not the blue car that appears in the picture. To do so, make sure the **Contiguous Area Only** check box is checked before clicking the sky with the tool.

Selecting the Entire Image
To select the entire image, open the **Mask** menu and choose **All**.

Trash Can Tool
Click the **Trash Can** tool (bottom-right on the Tools palette) to remove the mask and restore the underlying image.

(5) To invert the selection (so you can work with the area *outside* the dotted lines rather than *inside*), open the **Mask** menu and choose **Invert**.

(6) To move the mask (but not the image underneath), click the **Mask Move** tool. Then click inside the mask, drag the mask to move it, and release the mouse button.

(7) To move the portion of the image you selected with the mask, select the **Area Move** tool, click inside the mask, drag, and release the mouse button.

(8) To remove the mask, open the **Mask** menu and choose **None**.

End Task

Task 12: Using the Color Palette

Start Here

Use the Color palette to select the colors you want to apply to your image. The palette's colors change depending on the type of image you are working on. In other words, if you're working on a 24-bit **RGB** image, the palette will look different from when you're working with a 1-bit black-and-white image.

✓ **RGB Values**

RGB is a color model (that is, a system for describing colors) that describes a color in terms of its quantities of red, green, and blue. As you hover over a color in the Color palette, the status bar displays the RGB *color value* of the color under the pointer. In the RGB color model, each color's color value consists of three numbers ranging from 0 to 255 (each number represents the prominence of red, green, and blue in the given color). So, for example, the color value for pure red would be 255,0,0 (all red, no blue, no green).

1

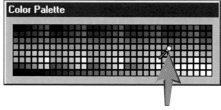

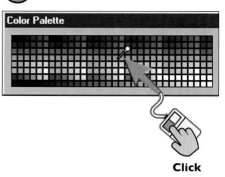
2

Click

1 Hover your mouse pointer over the Color palette; notice that your pointer changes to the Eyedropper tool's pointer.

2 Click to select the active color.

Next Step

Click

③ Click the alternative color in the Tools palette to make it the active color.

✓ **Active Color**
The active color—the one that is forward in the Tools palette—is the color that will be used for all painting and drawing tools. That is, if you were to apply the Bucket Fill tool to a selected area, that area would be covered with the active color.

✓ **Alternative Color**
The color behind the active color in the Tools palette is called the *alternative color*. Some tools, such as the Gradient tool, use this color, but more than anything, it's convenient to store a color that you think might make a good active color later on.

Task 13: Using PhotoStudio's Paint Tools

PhotoStudio provides several paint tools that you can use on your images.

Start Here

Click

Click

Click

✓ **Gradient Fill**
To apply a gradient fill to a selected area, as shown here, you must first use a selection tool.

✓ **Brush Palette**
Use the Brush palette to change the size of the brush point (measured in pixels), and the speed at which the various brush tools add their effects to your image when you move the mouse. You can also select a brush shape, or define your own by double-clicking the large button with the × on it. For more information about creating your own brush styles, see PhotoStudio's Help (you'll learn how to use Help later in this part).

If the Brush palette is not visible on your screen, open the **View** menu and select **Show Brush Palette**.

 Use the **Gradient Fill** tool to fill the selected area with a gradual blend from the alternative color (in this case, blue) to the active color (in this case, green).

 Use the **Bucket Fill** tool to fill the area you click with the active color, based on color similarity.

 Simulate airbrushing with the active color using the **Airbrush** tool.

Next Step

④ Use the **Paintbrush** tool to simulate—you guessed it—painting.

⑤ Use the **Smudge** tool to simulate the effect of smearing the image with your finger.

⑥ The **Pen** tool "paints" like a pen.

Task 14: Undoing Changes

There are two ways to undo changes you make to your images: using the **Undo** command under the **Edit** menu, or using the **Restore** command under the **File** menu. Use the Undo command to undo only the last change you've made; use the Restore command to restore your image file to its original state (that is, to the way it appeared when you opened it).

Start Here

Click

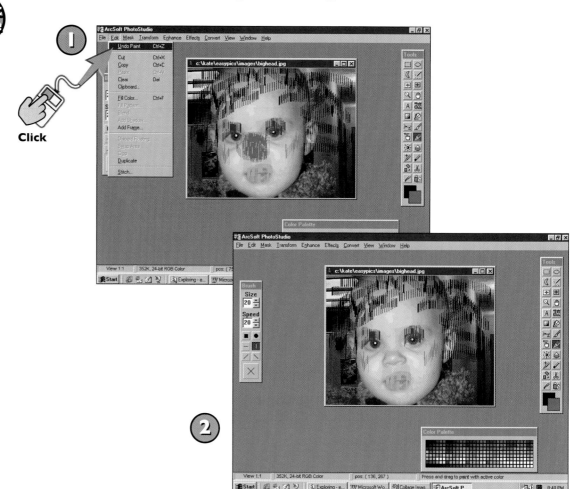

✓ **Undo/Redo**
When you undo a change, the Undo command changes to the Redo command. This is nice, in that if you want to "undo your undo," you can easily do so. On the downside, this means you can only undo one change to your file; if you want to undo the effect you applied three changes ago, you're out of luck.

① Open the **Edit** menu and choose **Undo**.

② The last effect you applied is removed.

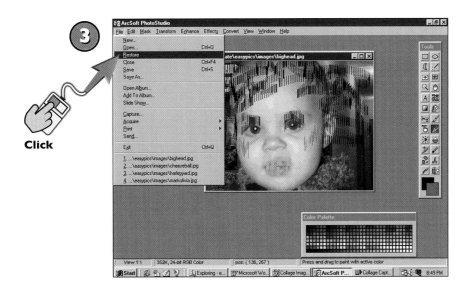

Click

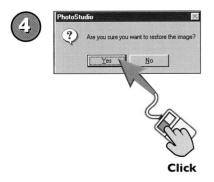

Click

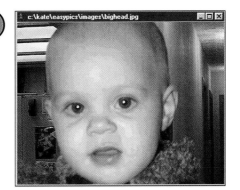

---

3 Open the **File** menu and choose **Restore**.

4 Confirm that you want to restore the image by clicking **Yes**.

5 The image is restored.

Task 15: Copying, Cutting, and Pasting

Sometimes you'll want to cut or copy all or part of your images. When you cut or copy an image, you add it to the *Clipboard*, a temporary storage space in your computer's memory. The Clipboard can hold only one selection at a time; if you cut or copy something new, the old selection is erased.

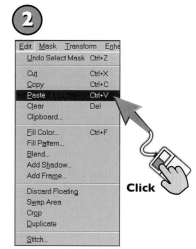

✓ **Unlimited Paste**
You can paste something that you've cut or copied an unlimited number of times (provided you don't replace the selection in the Clipboard with something new).

1 Use any selection tool to select the part of the image you want to copy, and then open the **Edit** menu and choose **Copy**.

2 Click the window containing the image, and then open the **Edit** menu and choose **Paste**.

3 The portion of the image that you copied is pasted in the upper-left corner of the image window.

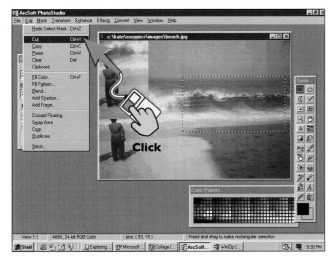

Click

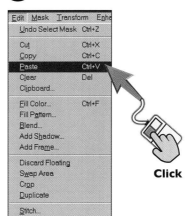

Click

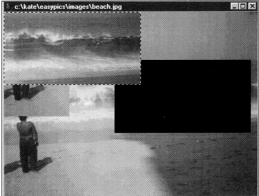

Select the part of the image you want to cut, open the **Edit** menu, and choose **Cut**.

Click the window containing the image, and then open the **Edit** menu and choose **Paste**.

The area you cut is pasted in the upper-left corner of the image, leaving a gap where it formerly appeared.

✅ **The Clear Command**
To clear the selected area (or the entire image if there is no selection) without adding it into the Clipboard, open the **Edit** menu and select **Clear**. After the image is cleared, the area where it formerly appeared is filled with the active color.

Task 16: Printing Images

There's something special about printed photographs: You can tuck them in your wallet, put them in your brag book, or frame them on the wall. Printing your images using PhotoStudio is simple.

Kodak Picture Maker
Some camera stores feature Kodak Picture Makers, which are self-service printers that enable you to make prints from existing prints, slides, negatives, PhotoCD discs, digital camera memory cards, or floppy disks. Before you print, you can use the touch-sensitive screen to edit the image, including zooming and cropping, using red-eye reduction, adjusting the color and density of the image, and adding mattes and borders.

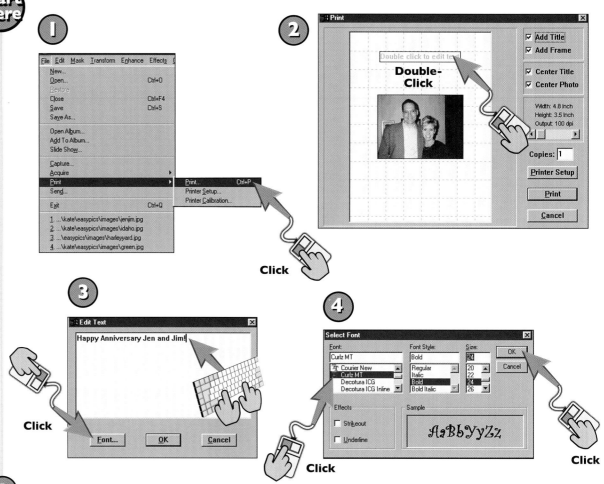

Start Here

Double-Click

Click

Click

Click

Click

With the image you want to print open on the PhotoStudio desktop, open the **File** menu, choose **Print**, and select **Print** from the submenu.

The **Add Title** check box is checked by default; to add text to the printout, double-click the text field in the preview area.

Type the text you want to add, and click the **Font** button.

Select a font, font style, and font size, and click **OK**. Click **OK** again, this time in the Edit Text dialog box.

Next Step

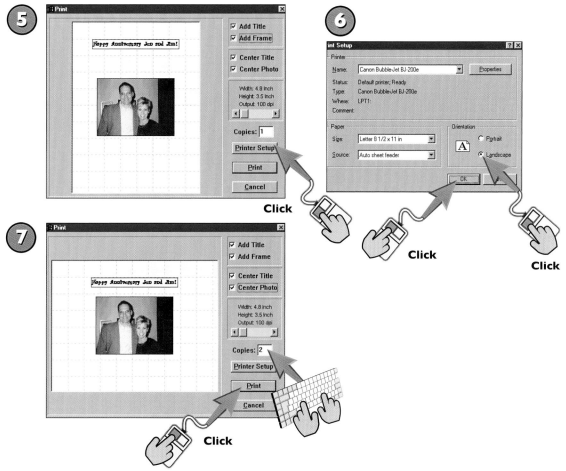

Paper Types
If you print on special photographic printing paper, which is coated, glossy, and heavy, your images will more closely resemble real photographs. To see what types of paper are available, shop around on the Web or check out your local office-supply store.

Adjusting the Size
You can adjust the size of the image on the page using the slider bar.

Moving the Image
To move the image on the page, click it and drag it to the spot on the page where you want it. (Note that the Center Photo check box is automatically unchecked.)

T-shirt Iron-On
You aren't limited to printing on paper; you can purchase special T-shirt iron-on paper to print on! Check your local office supply store for the paper you need.

⑤ The text is added. Click the **Printer Setup** button.

⑥ If desired, change the paper size and orientation (I've selected **Landscape**). Then click **OK**.

⑦ Specify the number of copies you want to print, and click **Print**.

Task 17: Color-Calibrating Your Printer for Digital Imaging

As your image passes from your monitor to your printer, you might notice that the colors in the image shift; this is because each device has its own way of defining and displaying colors. You can narrow the gap in the way colors are displayed by color-calibrating your system. Begin by printing your image; if you're satisfied with it, no need to calibrate! If, however, you notice that the reds are a little strong or the greens are a little weak, you can use PhotoStudio's printer calibration mapping function to tweak your system.

✓ RGB Versus CMYK

Unlike your monitor, which uses the RGB color system to display color, your printer uses a system called CMYK (cyan, magenta, yellow, and black). That means that the RGB color must be converted to CMYK, and that process isn't perfect. You might just need to learn to live with the slight discrepancy in colors.

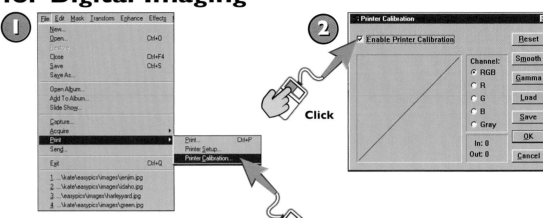

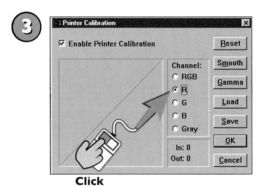

1   In PhotoStudio, open the **File** menu, choose **Print**, and select **Printer Calibration**.

2   Check the **Enable Printer Calibration** check box.

3   Select a channel from the **Channel** area. If you're adjusting a single RGB color, select that color.

Next Step ▶

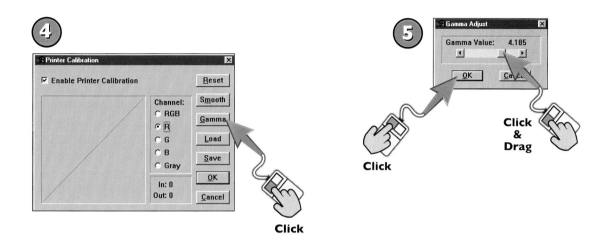

4

5

Click

Click
&
Drag

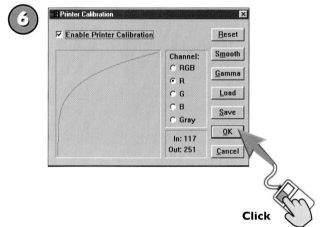

6

Click

(4) Click the **Gamma** button.

(5) Drag the slider or click the arrow buttons to adjust the gamma value. Click **OK**.

(6) The mapping curve is adjusted. Click **OK**, and then print the image to view the changes in the printer calibration. Repeat as needed.

✓ **Gamma Value**
Gamma refers to the overall brightness of the colors in an image. The higher the gamma value, the brighter the color.

✓ **Mapping Curve**
The mapping curve specifies how the color values are mapped to the printer. You can bypass clicking the Gamma button to adjust the curve by clicking and dragging the curve as needed.

✓ **Saving the Curve**
You can save the settings in the Printer Calibration dialog box by clicking the Save button. When you do, the Save Calibration Curve dialog box appears; save the file containing the curves as normal (note the .cal extension). To load a previously saved setting, click the **Load** button to open the Load Calibration Curve dialog box; find the file containing the settings, and open it as normal.

End Task

Task 18: Getting Help with PhotoStudio

No doubt there will be times when you need help with something that this book doesn't cover. When this happens, try using PhotoStudio's Help program. It's actually pretty useful and easy to use.

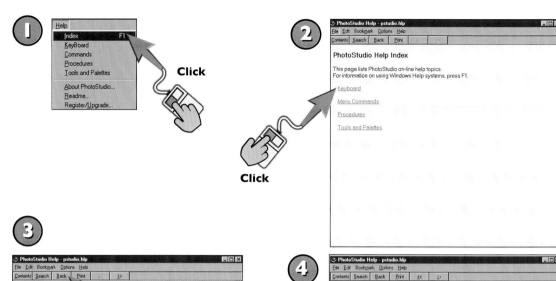

Click

Click

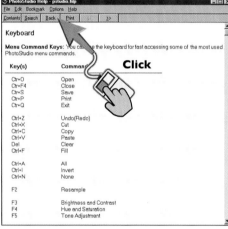

Click

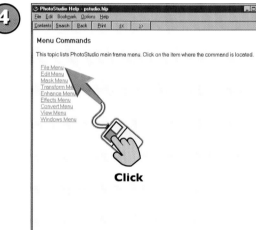

Click

1 Open the **Help** menu and choose **Index**.

2 The PhotoStudio Help Index window appears. Click the **Keyboard** link.

3 A page listing keyboard command shortcuts appears. Click **Back** to return to the PhotoStudio Help Index window.

4 Click the **Menu Commands** link to view a list of menus; click a menu link (in this case, **File Menu**) to view that menu's commands.

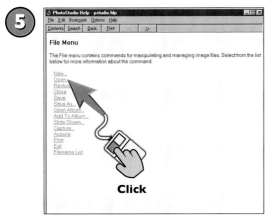

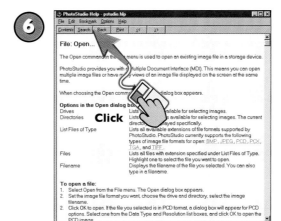

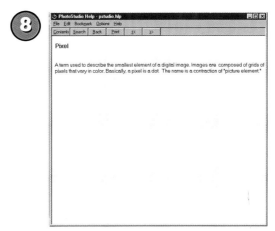

Printing Help
To print a Help page, click the **Print** button in the Help window. A standard Windows Print dialog box appears; proceed as normal.

Bookmarking Help
To bookmark a particular Help page so that you can easily revisit it, open that page, open the **Bookmark** menu, and select **Define**. Then, in the Bookmark Define dialog box, give the bookmark a name and click **OK**. The next time you want to revisit that page, open the **Bookmark** menu; the name you gave the bookmark will appear in the menu. Click it to view the page.

(5) A new page showing all the commands in the File menu appears. Click a command link (in this example, **Open**) to learn about that command.

(6) PhotoStudio's Help system displays information about the selected command. To search for specific information, click **Search**.

(7) Type the word you're looking for; PhotoStudio automatically selects it if it's in the index. Click **Display**.

(8) Information about the topic you typed is displayed.

Task 19: Closing Images

When you're finished working with an image, you'll want to close it to clear your desktop. Doing so is easy; this task shows you how.

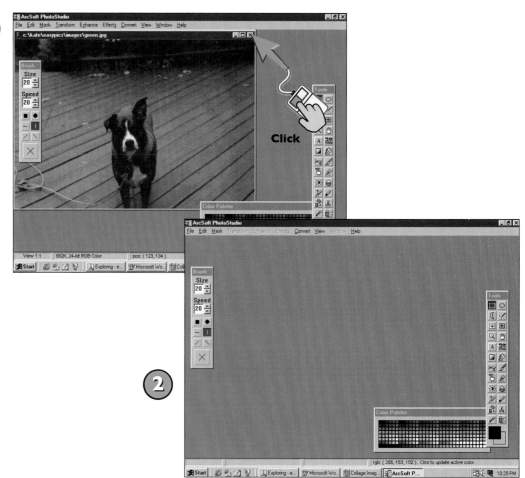

Click

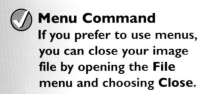 **Menu Command**
If you prefer to use menus, you can close your image file by opening the **File** menu and choosing **Close**.

Saving
If you've made changes to your image since saving it last, you'll be asked whether you want to save the newly changed image. Click **Yes**, **No**, or **Cancel** to continue closing the image.

 Click the **Close** (**X**) button in the upper-right corner of the image's window.

 The file is closed.

End Task

Task 20: Closing PhotoStudio

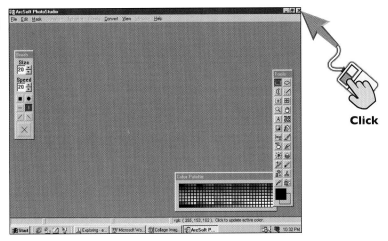

Click

When you're finished working with **PhotoStudio,** you'll want to close it to free up your computer's resources for other tasks.

1 Click the **Close (X)** button in the upper-right corner of the PhotoStudio desktop window.

2 PhotoStudio is closed.

 Menu Command
If you prefer to use menus, you can close your image file by opening the **File** menu and choosing **Exit.**

Touching Up Your Images with PhotoStudio

Those shoeboxes stuffed in your closet are probably full of photo disasters. You know the ones: Uncle Ed with the telephone pole growing out of his head, your sweet grandmother with demonic red eyes, you with your ex-boyfriend. What if you could correct those photo mistakes?

You can. Using ArcSoft's PhotoStudio, you can easily sharpen those out-of-focus photo gems, adjust for lousy lighting, restore Grandma's eyes to their normal hue, and even crop your ex. This chapter shows you how.

Tasks

Task 1: Sharpening Images

Everybody has pictures that would be spectacular—if only they were in focus. Fortunately, those near misses don't need to keep gathering dust in the closet; you can easily sharpen an image's focus using PhotoStudio!

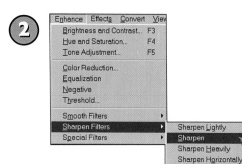

Click

✓ **Opening Files**
If you need help opening files, refer to Task 1, "Starting PhotoStudio," in Part 3, "PhotoStudio Basics."

✓ **Sharpening**
Use the **Sharpen Horizontally** and **Sharpen Vertically** commands to sharpen the image in a straight-across or up-and-down fashion, respectively. Using these commands is helpful for sharpening lines that move in a particular direction across the screen.

① Open the file containing the image that needs sharpening.

② Open the **Enhance** menu, choose **Sharpen Filters**, and choose **Sharpen Lightly**, **Sharpen**, or **Sharpen Heavily**, depending on your needs.

③ The image is sharpened.

End Task

Task 2: Cropping Images

Start Here

1

2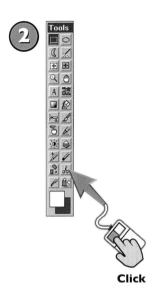

Click

You'll be amazed at how much cropping can do for an image! Whether you want to remove a person or an object or just alter the shape of the image for effect, cropping is the way to go. This task shows you how.

3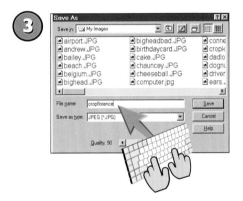

1 Open the file containing the image that needs to be cropped, and select the portion of the image that you want to crop to.

2 Click the **Crop Tool** button (the one with scissors on it) to create a new image document containing only the selected area of the image.

3 To save the cropped image, open the **File** menu and choose **Save As**. Locate the spot on your hard drive where you want to save the image, name it, and click **Save**.

 Selecting
Although you'll probably use the Rectangle Select tool to select what part of your image you want to crop to, don't forget that the Ellipse Select and Freehand Select tools will work as well. Using these tools enables you to crop your images in some really interesting ways. For more information about selecting portions of your image, see Task 11, "Using Selection Tools," of Part 3.

Task 3: Adjusting Brightness and Contrast

Start
Here!

Sometimes your pictures might come out too light or too dark. Fortunately, you can often correct this by using various tools in PhotoStudio's arsenal. For example, PhotoStudio enables you to adjust an image's brightness and contrast; this task shows you how.

Click

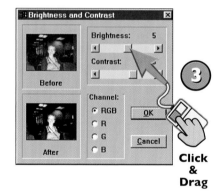

Click
&
Drag

✓ Adjusting Part of an Image

PhotoStudio enables you to apply the Brightness and Contrast tool either to your entire image or to a portion of an image. To apply this tool to only a portion of your image, use one of the selection tools to select the part you want to fix, and apply the tool as normal.

1 Open the file containing the image in which the lighting needs to be adjusted.

2 Open the **Enhance** menu and choose **Brightness and Contrast**.

3 Move the **Brightness** scrollbar to the left (darken) or right (brighten). Use the **After** pane to check the results.

Next
Step

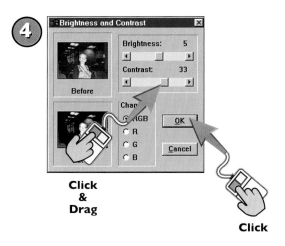

**Click
&
Drag**

Click

c:\my documents\my images\airport.jpg

 Channels

Although your image appears to contain lots of colors, it in fact contains only three: red, green, and blue (this color scheme is called *RGB*). Each of these colors is a *channel*. The Channel area of the Brightness and Contrast dialog box enables you to control which channels in the image are affected by your adjustments to the brightness and contrast. If you want to adjust only one color channel, select **R** (red), **G** (green), or **B** (blue). To adjust all three color channels at once (which is probably adequate for our needs), leave **RGB** selected.

 Tone Adjustment

Another way to adjust the brightness and contrast of your image is to use the **Enhance** menu's **Tone Adjustment** command. Using this command gives you much finer control, but is also slightly more complicated. See Task 5, "Enhancing an Image's Tone," for details.

4 Move the **Contrast** scrollbar to the left to blur the image or to the right to sharpen it. Again, use the **After** pane to check the results, and choose **OK**.

5 The brightness and contrast are adjusted. Repeat as necessary.

Task 4: Adjusting Hue and Saturation

When you adjust the tint and color on your TV, you are, in reality, adjusting its *hue*. When this happens, you are actually changing the colors on your set to new colors that are a particular number of degrees around the color wheel from the original color. The same thing happens when you adjust an image's hue and saturation. You can use the **Hue and Saturation** tool to adjust the intensity of the colors in your image.

Click

Click

 **Adjusting Part of an Image**

You can apply the **Hue and Saturation** tool either to all or part of your image. To apply it to only a part of your image, use one of the selection tools to select the part you want to adjust, and apply the tool as normal.

 Open the file containing the image in which the hue and saturation needs to be adjusted.

 Open the **Enhance** menu and choose **Hue and Saturation**.

 Move the **Hue** scrollbar to change the image's hue. Use the **Before** and **After** panes to check the results.

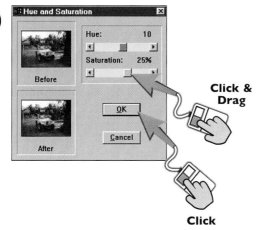

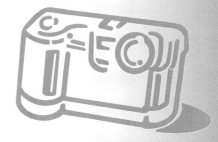

**Click &
Drag**

Click

Move the **Saturation** scrollbar to the right or left to make colors more or less intense. When you're satisfied with the image in the **After** pane, choose **OK**.

The hue and saturation are adjusted. Repeat as necessary.

Task 5: Enhancing an Image's Tone

Start Here

The Tone Adjustment command is similar to the Brightness and Contrast command, but a bit more involved. You can use the Tone Adjustment command to control the lightness or darkness of the image's highlights, midtones, and shadows.

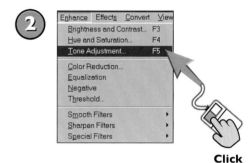

Click

✓ Histogram and Mapping Curve

The Tone Adjustment dialog box contains two tools that can help you adjust your image's tone: the histogram (a special type of line chart that shows the color distributions of an image) and the mapping curve (this shows current color intensities versus new ones).

1 Open the file containing the image in which the tone needs to be adjusted.

2 Open the **Enhance** menu and choose **Tone Adjustment**.

Next Step

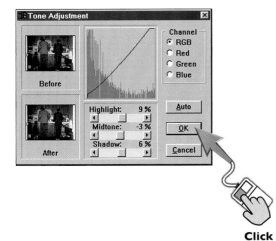

Before

After

Tone Adjustment

Channel
- RGB
- Red
- Green
- Blue

Highlight: 9 %
Midtone: -3 %
Shadow: 6 %

Auto

OK

Cancel

Click

c:\my documents\my images\kitchenscout.jpg

Adjust the **Highlight**, **Midtone**, and **Shadow** scrollbars until you're satisfied with the preview image, and then choose **OK**.

The tone is adjusted. Repeat as necessary.

 The Auto Button
Click the **Auto** button in the Tone Adjustment dialog box to automatically alter the highlight or shadow functions for optimal results.

Task 6: Editing Out Eyesores

After receiving proofs of our wedding pictures from the photographer, we chose to enlarge our favorite photo to an 8×10. Imagine our surprise when the enlarged print revealed something we hadn't noticed before: an enormous **INSECT**. When I pointed it out to the photographer, she realized that somehow, somewhere, a bug had become embedded in the negative. Although your photos might not have insects on them, some no doubt have other eyesores. Fortunately, you can use PhotoStudio to cover them up.

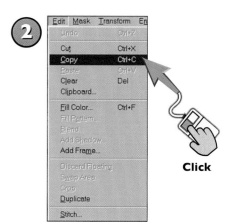

Click

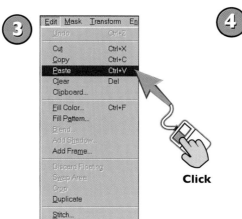

Click

Click

Because the bug appears where grass is supposed to be, I'll begin by using the **Ellipse Select** tool to select grass from another section of the photo.

Open the **Edit** menu and choose **Copy**.

Click the image, and then open the **Edit** menu and choose **Paste**.

The circle of grass I copied appears in the top-left corner of the image window.

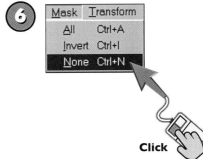

Click

Using the **Area Move** tool, click and drag the grass into place.

Remove the mask around the grass by opening the **Mask** menu and choosing **None**.

Task 7: Eliminating Red Eye

Nothing can ruin a photo more than when the subject's eyes turn that demonic shade of red. Fortunately, you can restore your subject's baby blues using PhotoStudio.

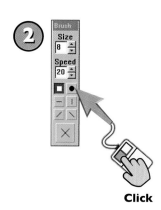

Click

Click

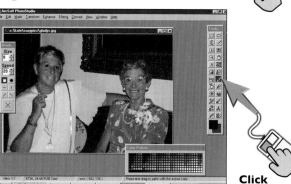

Click

Click

No Color Palette?
If your screen doesn't have a Color palette on it, open the **View** menu and choose **Show Color Palette.**

① From the Color palette, select the color you want to use to replace the red in the eye.

② In the Brush toolbar, click the **Circle** button. (You might also consider lowering the value in the **Size** field to make the brush smaller.)

③ Using the **Paintbrush** tool, click to replace the red with the color you selected.

④ Repeat step 3, but on the other eye.

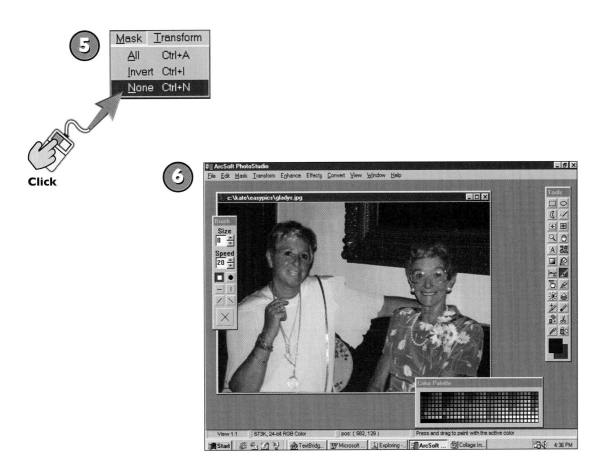

Click

Mask Transform
All   Ctrl+A
Invert   Ctrl+I
None   Ctrl+N

---

5 Open the **Mask** menu and choose **None**.

6 Goodbye red eye!

Task 8: Airbrushing Glare from Glasses

If you've ever used a flash when photographing someone with glasses, you know how the glare from the flash can mar your finished product. Removing glare is a lot like removing red eye; this task shows you how.

Start Here

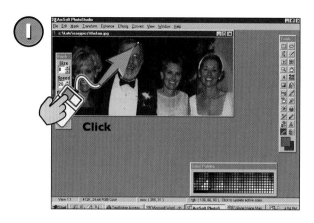

Click

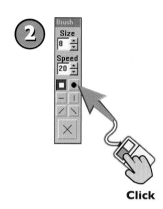

Click

Click

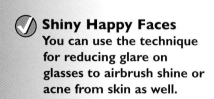

Shiny Happy Faces
You can use the technique for reducing glare on glasses to airbrush shine or acne from skin as well.

1. Using the **Eyedropper** tool, click the person's face to get a skin tone match (the forehead's a good place).

2. In the Brush toolbar, click the **Circle** button. (You might also consider lowering the value in the **Size** field.)

3. Using the **Airbrush** tool, click the glare to replace it with the skin-tone color (you might have to click a few times to cover it completely).

Next Step

4 Repeat step 3, but this time remove the glare on the other lens.

5 The lenses look glare-free!

Task 9: Adding a White Border to Your Photo

If you like your photographs to be surrounded by a white border, you can easily add one. This task shows you how.

Click

Click

 Open the image you want to add a border to. Then, in the Color palette, click the white tile to specify white as the active color.

 Open the **Edit** menu and choose **Add Frame**.

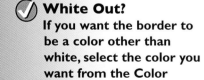

White Out?

If you want the border to be a color other than white, select the color you want from the Color palette.

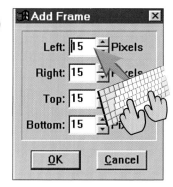

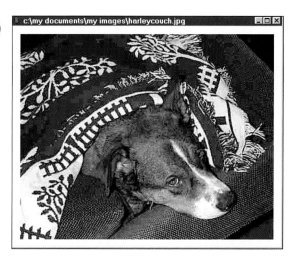

③ Using either the arrow buttons or your keyboard, specify how many pixels wide the border should be (15 is a good number). Then choose **OK**.

④ The border is added.

Applying Special Effects

ArcSoft's PhotoStudio software has several filters that you can apply to your image for various effects. Want to tweak your image to resemble an oil painting? Simply apply the Oil Painting filter! Curious to see how your image would look if it was embossed? Apply the Emboss filter. This part guides you through the use of PhotoStudio's coolest filters.

Tasks

Just because you don't have the skills of Claude Monet doesn't mean you can't make your images look like oil paintings. PhotoStudio provides a filter that enables you to do just that.

Task 1: Making Your Image Resemble an Oil Painting

Start Here

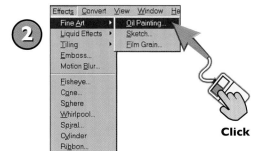

Click

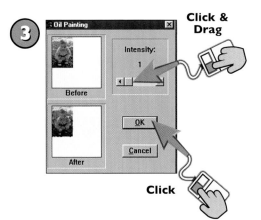

Click & Drag

Click

Click

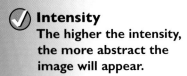
✓ **Intensity**
The higher the intensity, the more abstract the image will appear.

① Open the image that you want to alter to resemble an oil painting.

② Open the **Effects** menu, choose **Fine Art**, and click **Oil Painting**.

③ Adjust the intensity of the Oil Painting filter by dragging the slider. When you're satisfied with the image, choose **OK**.

④ Voilà! The filter is applied.

End Task

Task 2: Altering Your Image to Resemble a Sketch

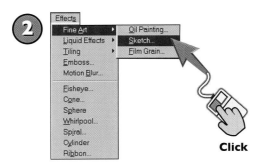

Click

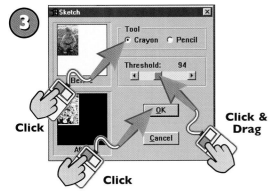

Click

Click

**Click &
Drag**

Why waste time sketching from your photos when you can simply apply the Sketch filter? You can easily alter your image to resemble a pencil sketch or a crayon sketch. Sketchbook not required.

(1) Open the image that you want to alter to resemble a sketch.

(2) Open the **Effects** menu, choose **Fine Art**, and click **Sketch**.

(3) In the Sketch dialog box, select whether you want a pencil sketch or a crayon sketch, adjust the threshold, and choose **OK**.

(4) The filter is applied.

End Task

Applying a film-grain effect to an image can make the image appear—well—grainier. This effect is nice if you're trying to make your image appear retro or more "industrial."

Task 3: Applying a Film Grain to Your Image

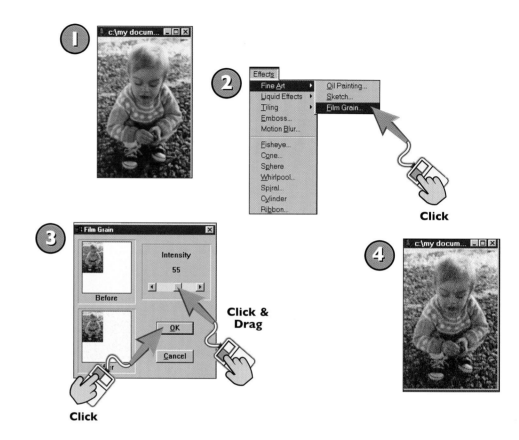

Click

**Click &
Drag**

Click

(1) Open the image to which you want to apply a film grain.

(2) Open the **Effects** menu, choose **Fine Art**, and click **Film Grain**.

(3) In the Film Grain dialog box, adjust the intensity of the grain, and choose **OK**.

(4) The filter is applied.

Task 4: Applying a Splash Filter

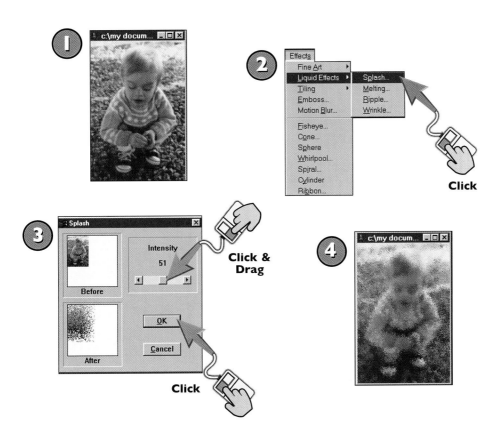

Click

Click & Drag

Click

Just in case you ever want to alter your image to look as though it is covered with frosty shower glass, PhotoStudio has the filter for you: the Splash filter. This task shows you how to use it.

1. Open the image to which you want to apply the Splash filter.

2. Open the **Effects** menu, choose **Liquid Effects**, and click **Splash**.

3. In the Splash dialog box, adjust the intensity of the splash, and choose **OK**.

4. The filter is applied.

Task 5: Applying a Melting Effect

When you apply the
Melting filter, your image
appears to be, well, melting.
This filter can add some
fascinating effects to
landscapes and objects that
have interesting colors or
textures, and can make
your portraits look pretty
cool in that *Raiders of the
Lost Ark*, people's-faces-are-
melting-off kind of way.

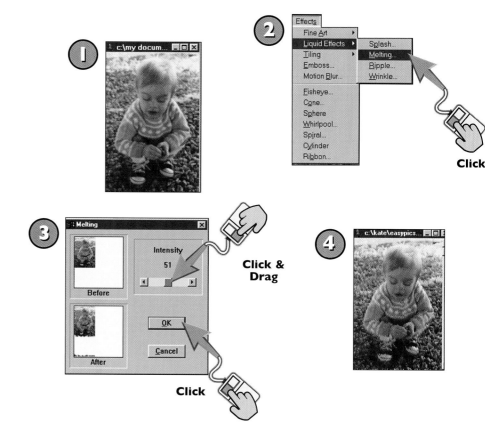

① Open the image to which you want to apply the Melting filter.

② Open the **Effects** menu, choose **Liquid Effects**, and click **Melting**.

③ In the Melting dialog box, adjust the intensity of the melt, and choose **OK**.

④ The filter is applied.

Task 6: Applying a Ripple Effect

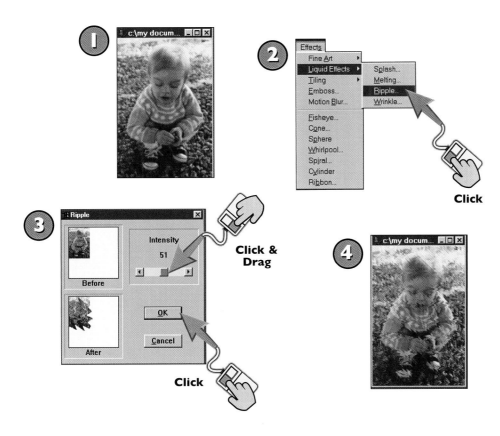

If you want your image to appear rippled, the Ripple filter is just the tool you need. When you apply the Ripple filter, your image looks a lot like it would if it were reflected in water.

1. Open the image to which you want to apply the Ripple filter.

2. Open the **Effects** menu, choose **Liquid Effects**, and click **Ripple**.

3. Use the slider bar to adjust the intensity of the ripple, and choose **OK**.

4. The filter is applied.

Imagine that your image has been ironed onto a linen shirt...and now imagine that you've been wearing that linen shirt for days. This is the effect you'll get if you apply the Wrinkle filter to your picture.

Task 7: Applying a Wrinkle Effect

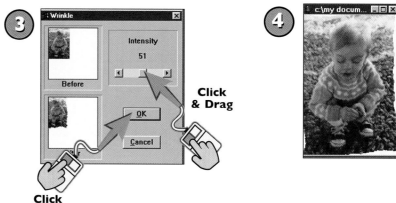

① Open the image to which you want to apply the Wrinkle filter.

② Open the **Effects** menu, choose **Liquid Effects**, and click **Wrinkle**.

③ Use the slider bar to adjust the intensity of the wrinkle, and choose **OK**.

④ The filter is applied.

Task 8: Creating a 3D Grid of Your Image

If you're wondering what your image would look like after being pressed in a waffle iron, have I got the tool for you: PhotoStudio's 3D Grid filter. Applying this filter is easy; you can even decide whether you want a Belgian waffle or a regular one.

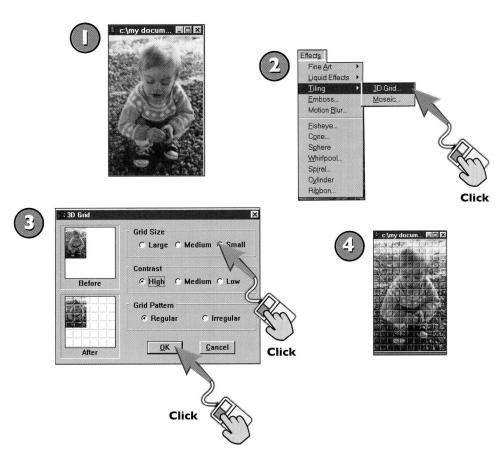

Click

Click

Click

1. Open the image to which you want to apply the 3D Grid filter.

2. Open the **Effects** menu, choose **Tiling**, and click **3D Grid**.

3. Specify the grid size, contrast, and pattern, and then choose **OK**.

4. The filter is applied.

Task 9: Tiling Your Image

In case you're wondering how your picture would look if it was tiled on a bus station wall, PhotoStudio has provided the Mosaic filter.

✓ **Tile Size**
The larger the tiles, the more abstract your image will become.

✓ **The Square Check Box**
If the **Square** check box in the Mosaic dialog box is checked, then adjusting either the **Width** or **Height** automatically adjusts the other.

✓ **PhotoMontage**
Don't confuse the Mosaic filter with PhotoMontage. PhotoMontage is a program that enables you to tile your image with zillions of smaller images, and is a whole lot cooler than the Mosaic filter in PhotoStudio! You'll learn how to use PhotoMontage later on in this part.

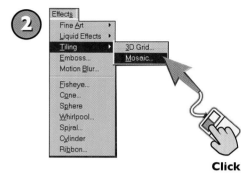

Click

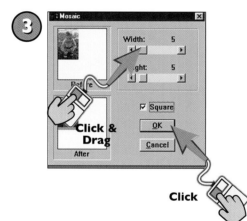

Click

1. Open the image to which you want to apply the Mosaic filter.

2. Open the **Effects** menu, choose **Tiling**, and click **Mosaic**.

3. Adjust the width and height of the tiles, and choose **OK**.

4. The filter is applied.

Task 10: Embossing Your Image

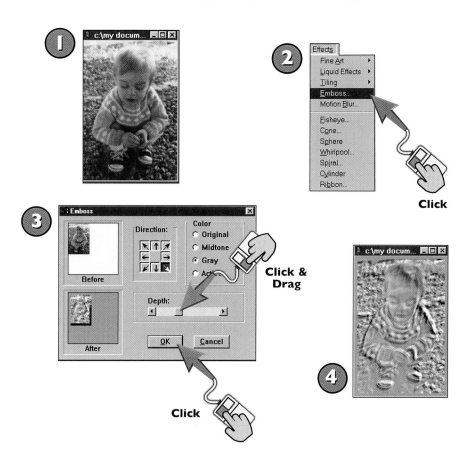

The Emboss filter provides an interesting effect, making your image appear raised up from or stamped into the background.

Open the image to which you want to apply the Emboss filter.

Open the **Effects** menu and choose **Emboss**.

Select the direction of the emboss, the color (gray is effective), and the depth (the higher the depth, the more pronounced the effect). Choose **OK**.

The filter is applied.

Task 11: Applying a Motion Blur

Start Here

Have a picture of your kid on his bike for the first time? Even though he barely made it down the street in one piece, let alone with any modicum of speed, you can make him look like **Speed Racer** in no time flat just by using PhotoStudio's **Motion Blur** filter. This task shows you how applying a Motion Blur filter can make even people who are standing still look like they're moving around.

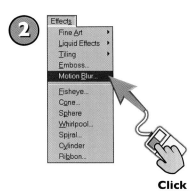

Click

① Open the image to which you want to apply the Motion Blur filter.

② Open the **Effects** menu and choose **Motion Blur**.

Next Step

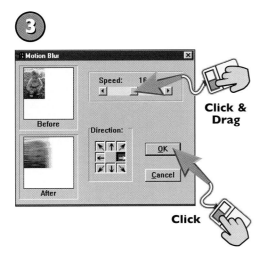

3) Select the speed and direction of the motion, and then choose **OK**.

4) The filter is applied.

Task 12: Applying Effects to Portions of Your Image

To apply a filter to only a portion of your image, you must use a *mask*. Think of masks as being like masking tape. When you want to paint only part of your wall, you use masking tape to "tape off" the area you want to paint. In PhotoStudio, you do the same thing: You use selection tools to "tape off" the part of the image you want to change.

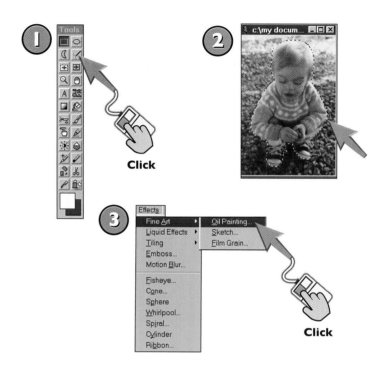

✅ **Masks**
For more information on using masks, refer to Part 3, "PhotoStudio Basics."

1 Click the **Freehand Select** tool in the toolbar.

2 Trace the portion of the image to which you want to apply the filter. When you finish outlining the mask, double-click to activate it.

3 Open the **Effects** menu, choose **Fine Art**, and click **Oil Painting**.

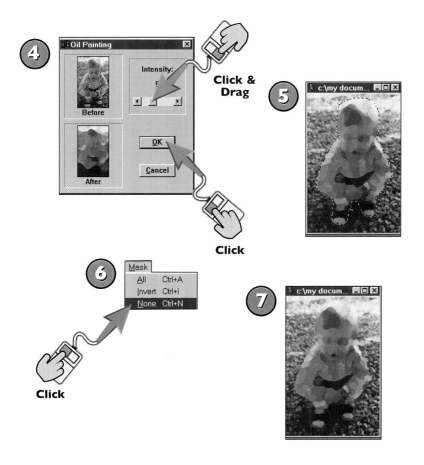

4 Adjust the effect's intensity by dragging the slider. When you're satisfied with the image, choose **OK**.

5 The filter is applied to the selected area only.

6 To remove the mask, open the **Mask** menu and choose **None**.

7 The dotted outline disappears, but the changes you made to the masked area remain intact.

Task 13: Adding Text to Your Image

You can easily add a line of text to your image using PhotoStudio's Text tool.

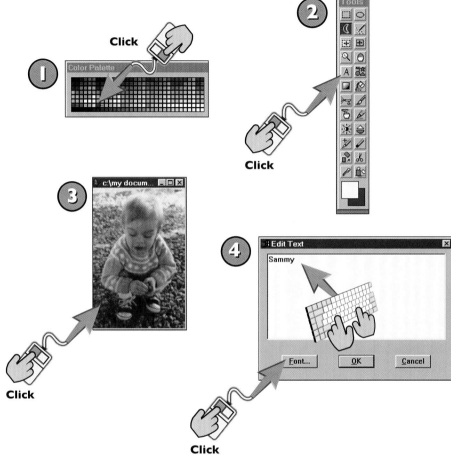

Click

Click

Click

Click

✅ **Where to Click**
After you decide where on the image you want the text to appear, click the top-left corner of that space for best results.

✅ **Multiple Lines**
To add multiple lines of text to your image, you must use the Text tool to create each line individually.

① Select the color you want your text to be by clicking it in the Color palette.

② Click the **Text** tool.

③ Click the spot on your image where you want the text to start.

④ The Edit Text window opens; type the text you want to appear on the image, and then click the **Font** button.

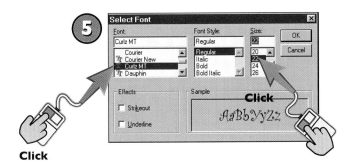

Click

Click

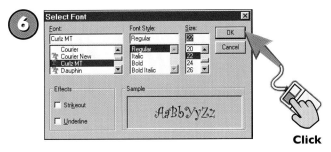

Click

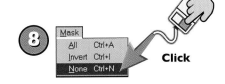

Click

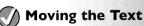

Moving the Text
To reposition the text on the image, use the **Area Move** tool (third from the top on the right side of the Tools panel). Simply click the tool on the text, and then, while holding down the mouse button, drag the text to the spot you want.

(5) Select the font, font style, font size, and any effects that you want to apply. Preview your selections in the Sample area.

(6) Choose **OK** in the Select Font dialog box, and again in the Edit Text dialog box.

(7) The text you created appears as a floating selection.

(8) To apply the text for good, open the **Mask** menu and choose **None**.

You might have a great image, but what if it has a lousy background? You can easily place the subject of your picture in a new, more interesting environment. This task shows you how.

Task 14: Changing Your Photo's Background

Double-Click

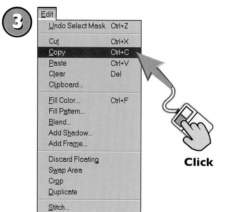

Click

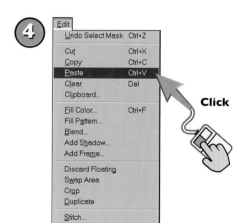

Click

① Open both the image file that contains the background you want to use and the image whose subject you want to place in the new background.

② Using the **Freehand Select** tool, trace your subject. Double-click to activate the mask.

③ Open the **Edit** menu and choose **Copy**.

④ Click the window containing the background image, and then open the **Edit** menu and choose **Paste**.

Next Step

Click

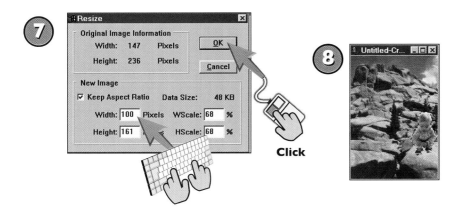

Click

✅ **Saving the New Image**
It's recommended that you save the new image as a separate file. That way, you'll still have copies of the originals. To do so, click the new image to select it, and then open the **File** menu and choose **Save As**. Navigate to the spot on your hard drive where you want to store the file, give the file a unique name (in this example, I've named the new file **Samrocks**), and choose **OK**.

✅ **Removing the Mask**
To remove the dotted outline of the mask from the image, open the **Mask** menu and choose **None**. The changes you made to the masked area still apply; only the outline disappears.

⑤ The image you copied is pasted into the background image.

⑥ To resize the pasted image so that it doesn't dwarf (or overwhelm) the background, open the **Transform** menu and choose **Resize**.

⑦ With **Keep Aspect Ratio** checked, enter a smaller (or larger) value in either the **Height** or **Width** field, and choose **OK**.

⑧ The image is resized. To adjust the placement of the copied image, click the **Area Move** tool and drag as needed.

Who can resist placing their dog's head on their kid's body? Or placing Richard Nixon's head on their dog's body? Or...You get the idea. PhotoStudio makes it easy to create images that deceive the eyes. Don't forget to call *Weekly World News* when you finish this task!

Task 15: Putting Your Dog's Head on Your Kid's Body

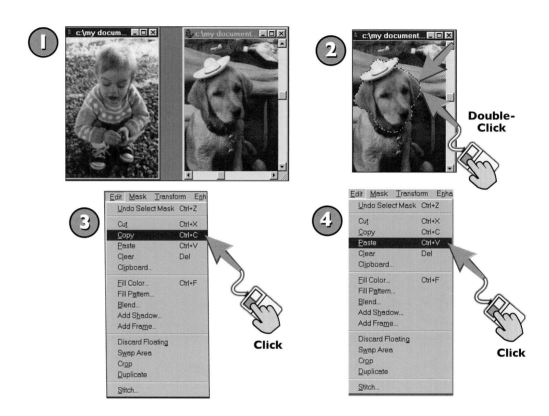

1 Open both the image file that contains your dog's head and the image file that contains your child's body.

2 Use the **Freehand Select** tool to trace your dog's head. When you finish, double-click to activate the mask.

3 Open the **Edit** menu and choose **Copy**.

4 Click the window containing your kid's image, and then open the **Edit** menu and choose **Paste**.

Next Step

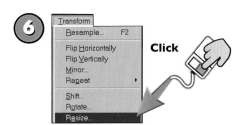

Click

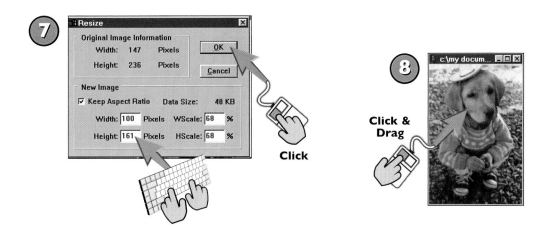

Click

Click

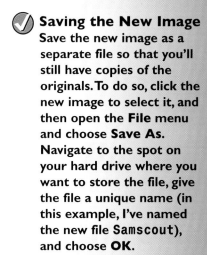

Click & Drag

✓ **Saving the New Image**
Save the new image as a separate file so that you'll still have copies of the originals. To do so, click the new image to select it, and then open the **File** menu and choose **Save As**. Navigate to the spot on your hard drive where you want to store the file, give the file a unique name (in this example, I've named the new file Samscout), and choose **OK**.

⑤ The dog's head is pasted into the file with your kid's body.

⑥ To resize the pasted image—in this case, so that the dog's head fully covers the child's—open the **Transform** menu and choose **Resize**.

⑦ With **Keep Aspect Ratio** checked, enter a new value in either the **Height** or **Width** field, and choose **OK**.

⑧ To adjust the placement of the resized image, click the **Area Move** tool and drag as needed. Then remove the mask (click **Mask** and select **None**).

Task 16: Stitching Photos Together

Everybody loves those panorama cameras that let you capture a wide-angle scene, but not everybody owns one. That's why PhotoStudio's Stitch feature comes in handy. Using it, you can easily "stitch" two photos together to create a single image, be it of the Grand Canyon, the grandkids, or both.

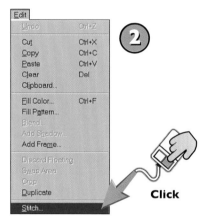

Click

✓ Stitching Candidates

Some photos stitch together better than others. When deciding what to stitch together, look for images with similar characteristics (for example, stitching together a close-up view of your kid with a long-distance view of a mountain can lead to problems, as you'll see in this task).

1 Open the images that you want to stitch together.

2 Open the **Edit** menu and choose **Stitch**.

Next Step

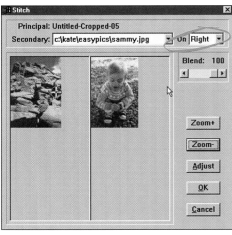

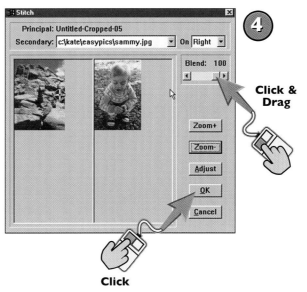

Click & Drag

Click

③ Use the **On** field to specify which image you want to appear on the left and which should be on the right.

④ Use the **Blend** slider to set the blend (the higher the setting, the heavier the blend), and choose **OK**.

⑤ The images are stitched together.

Mirroring your images can create interesting effects. PhotoStudio's Mirror feature enables you to mirror images in four directions: left, right, top, and bottom.

Task 17: Mirroring Images

Start Here

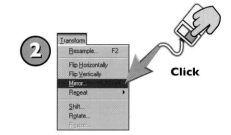
Click

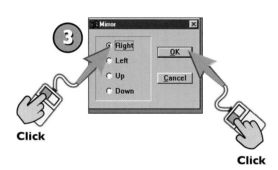

Click

Click

Open the image that you want to mirror.

Open the **Transform** menu and choose **Mirror**.

Specify the direction of the mirror and choose **OK**.

Twins! (You might need to expand the window to view the entire mirrored image.)

End Task

Task 18: Duplicating Images

Click

Duplicating an image is similar to mirroring an image except that (surprise) an exact copy is created instead of a mirror. PhotoStudio enables you to choose whether you want to copy the image vertically or horizontally.

1. Open the image that you want to duplicate.

2. Open the **Transform** menu, choose **Repeat**, and select either **Horizontally** or **Vertically**.

3. More twins! (Again, you might need to expand the window to view the entire mirrored image.)

Task 19: Using PhotoFantasy to Fool Your Friends

If you've ever wanted to fly to the moon, be on a baseball card, dunk like Michael Jordan, or be President of the United States, you'll love PhotoFantasy. Although it doesn't actually help you accomplish these goals, it at least makes it *look* like you have.

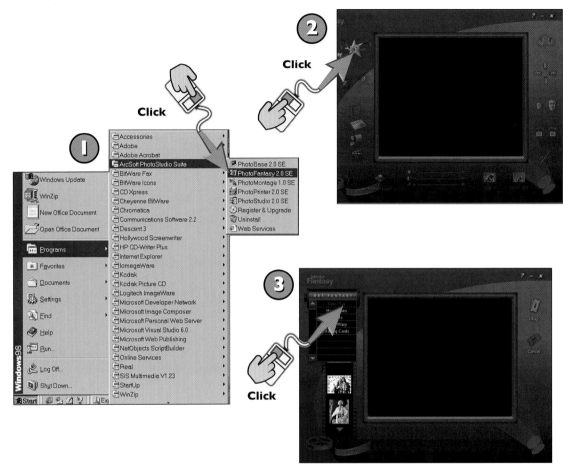

1. Click the **Start** button, choose **Programs**, select **ArcSoft PhotoStudio Suite**, and click **PhotoFantasy 2.0 SE**.

2. Click **Get Fantasy**.

3. Click the down-arrow button on the film roll and select a category (I've selected **Role Play**).

✓ PhotoFantasy CD
The CD that accompanies this book must be inserted in your CD-ROM drive for PhotoFantasy to work.

Next Step

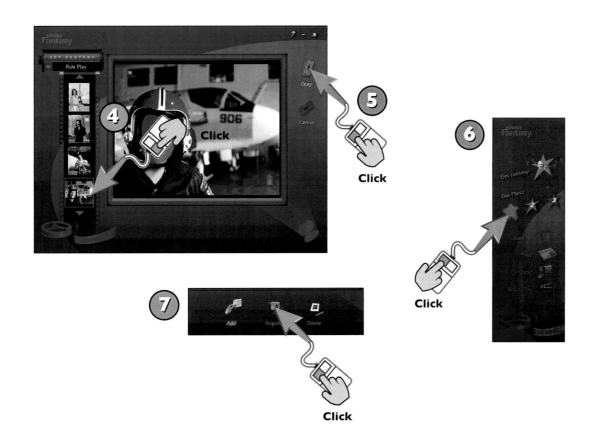

Click

Click

Click

Click

4 Use the arrows on each end of the filmstrip to scroll through the images. Click a thumbnail to see the full-screen version.

5 Choose **Okay** to select the image.

6 Click the blue star under **Get Photo**.

7 Because you want to use a picture of your own instead of a sample image, click the **Add** icon.

Next Step

Using PhotoFantasy to Fool Your Friends Continued

Click

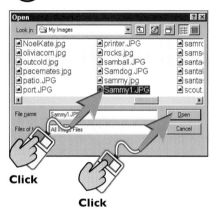

Click

Click

---

8 Using the standard Open dialog box, find the file you want to use, select it, and click **Open**.

9 The image you want appears; choose **Okay**.

10 The image you selected in step 8 appears in the photo you selected in step 4 (as you can see, the sizing and placement is a bit off).

Next Step

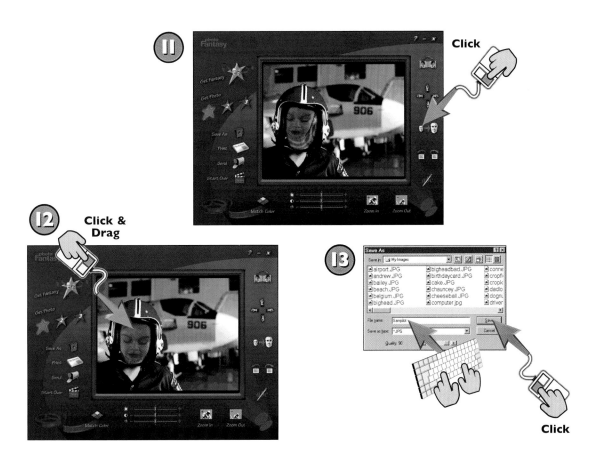

Click

Click & Drag

Click

⑪ To adjust the sizing, click and hold on the icon that resembles a mask.

⑫ After you get the sizing right, click and drag the face to move it into place.

⑬ Click **Save As**. In the Save As dialog box, navigate to the spot on your hard drive where you want to save the image, name the image, and click **Save**.

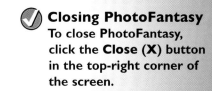

✅ **Closing PhotoFantasy**
To close PhotoFantasy, click the **Close (X)** button in the top-right corner of the screen.

End Task

Task 20: Using PhotoMontage

If you're a fan of *Star Wars*, you may have noticed those posters where the image of Darth Vader consists of zillions of tinier images from the movie. Well, with **PhotoMontage**, you can create similar images of your own!

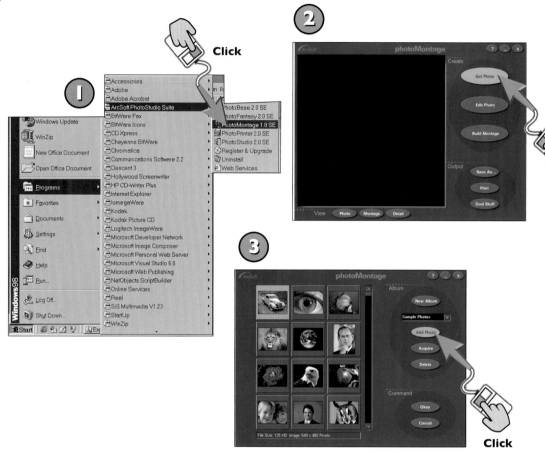

Click

Click

Click

1 Click the **Start** button, choose **Programs**, select **ArcSoft PhotoStudio Suite**, and click **PhotoMontage 1.0 SE**.

2 Click the **Get Photo** button.

3 To use one of your own photos instead of a sample one, click **Add Photo**.

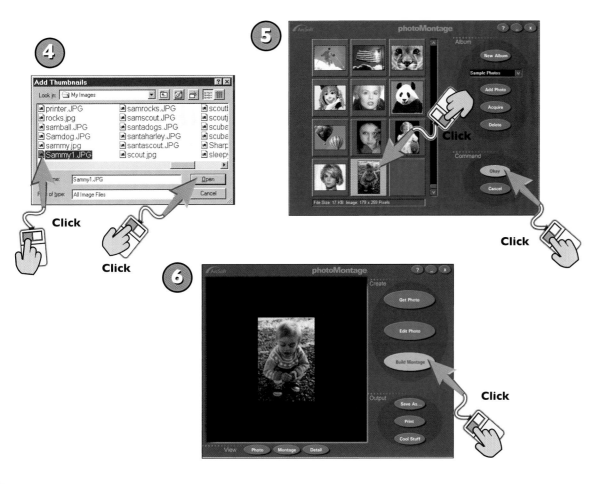

4. Find the file you want to use, select it, and click **Open**.

5. The image appears in the grid. Select it, and choose **Okay**.

6. If you need to edit the image (for example, if you want to crop it or adjust the brightness), click **Edit Photo**. Otherwise, click **Build Montage**.

Using PhotoMontage Continued

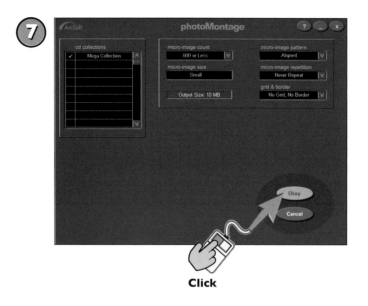

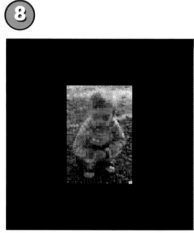

Click

7. Feel free to adjust the settings (although the defaults provide excellent results), and choose **Okay**.

8. It might take awhile, but the montage will be built.

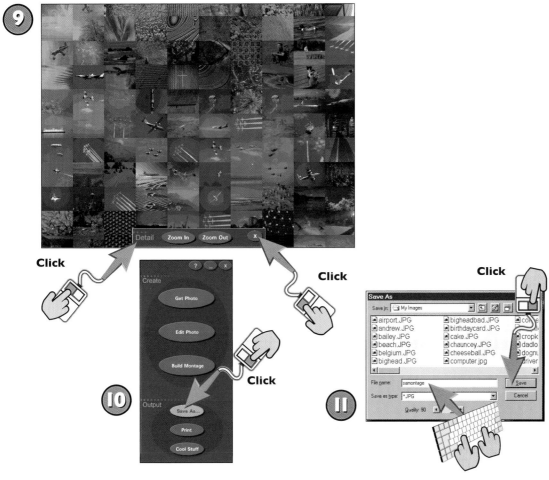

Click

Click

Click

Click

⑨ To see a detail of the montage, click **Detail**. To exit Detail view, click the **Close (X)** button.

⑩ To save the montage, click **Save As**.

⑪ Navigate to the spot on your hard drive where you want to save the image, name it, and click **Save**.

PART 6

Storing Digital Images Using PhotoStudio's Album Feature

If you're tired of stuffing pictures into shoeboxes and cramming them in your closets, this part is for you! Using PhotoStudio's album feature, you can easily organize and store your images, just as you would with a "real" photo album—without worrying about using acid-free paper.

Tasks

Task 1: Creating a New Photo Album to Store Your Images

Storing your images in PhotoStudio albums makes it easy to find the images you want to work with. This is especially handy if you're working on multiple projects that use different sets of images. For example, if one project consists of images of your grandparents and another project consists of images of your pets, you can create different albums for each set of image files. Then, you can use each album's thumbnails to quickly find and open the pictures you need.

☑️ **Sample Images**
PhotoStudio comes with a slew of sample images that you can play around with; you'll find these images in the Sample Images album.

☑️ **Album Storage**
Albums are stored as individual files with the .ABM extension in the C:\Program Files\ ArcSoft\PhotoStudio Suite\Ps_20se\Albums directory.

Start Here

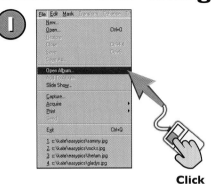

Click

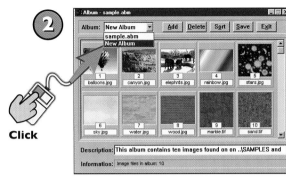

Click

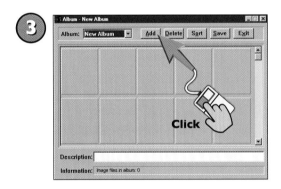

Click

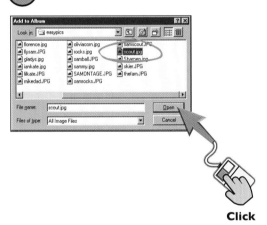

Click

(1) In PhotoStudio, open the **File** menu and choose **Open Album**.

(2) The open Album window displays thumbnails of images in the current album (**sample.abm**). To create a new album, open the **Album** drop-down list and choose **New Album**.

(3) The new album is created. To add your first image, click **Add**.

(4) Select the image you want to add, and click the **Open** button.

Next Step

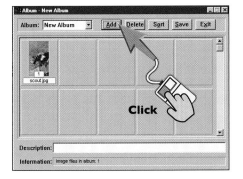

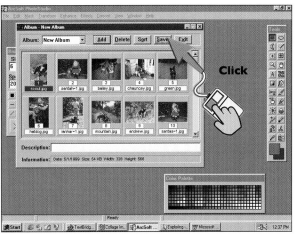

Click

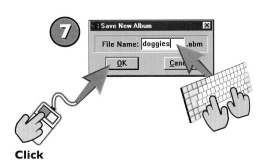

Click

Ctrl+Click
If you want to add multiple image files to your album, hold down the **Ctrl** key on your keyboard and click each file you want to open in the **Add to Album** dialog box. Click the **Open** button, and every file you select is added to the album.

Image Descriptions
Adding descriptions to your images, such as names or dates, can help jog your memory when you peruse your album. To do so, click the image to which you want to add a description. To select it, click in the **Description** field, and type the description.

Album Descriptions
You can also add a description for the entire album; to do so, click the album's name in the **Album** drop-down list, click in the **Description** field, and type the description.

5. The image is added. Repeat steps 3 and 4 until you've added all the pictures you want to the album.

6. After you've added all the images you want to the album, click the **Save** button.

7. Name the album in the **File Name** field of the Save New Album dialog box, and choose **OK**.

8. The album is saved with the name you specified.

End Task

Task 2: Opening an Existing Album

Opening an album that you've already created (or the Sample Images album) is easy; this task shows you how.

Start Here

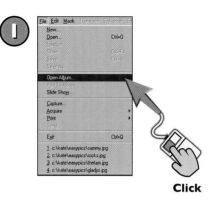

Click

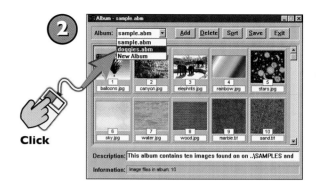

Click

---

1 Open the **File** menu and choose **Open Album**.

2 The open Album window displays images in the current album. To open a different album, choose it from the **Album** drop-down list.

3 The album you selected is opened.

End Task

Task 3: Adding Images to an Album

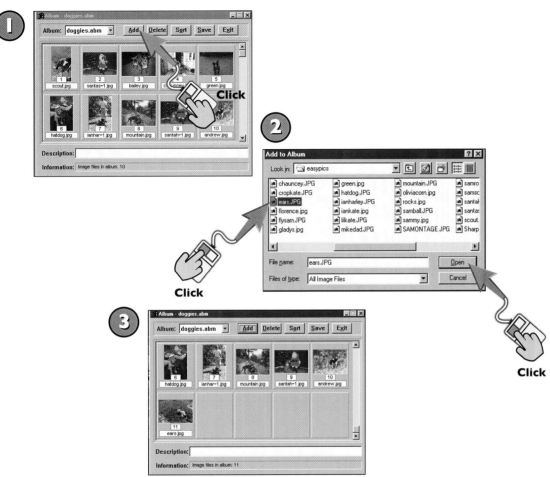

Click

①

②

③

Click

Click

Your albums are living documents; that is, you can always add and delete from existing albums. This task shows you how to add images; the next task shows you how to delete them.

 Ctrl+Click
If you want to add multiple image files to your album, hold down the **Ctrl** key on your keyboard and click each file you want to open in the **Add to Album** dialog box. Click the **Open** button and every file you select is added to the album.

 A Shortcut...
If the image you want to add to an album is currently open in PhotoStudio, you can add it without opening the album itself. To do so, open PhotoStudio's **File** menu, choose **Add to Album**, select the album you want in the **Add to Album** dialog box, and choose **OK**.

① Open the album to which you want to add images, and click the **Add** button.

② In the Add to Album dialog box, select the image file you want to add and click **Open**.

③ The image is added to the album.

Task 4: Deleting Images from an Album

Deleting images from your album is even easier than adding them; this task shows you how.

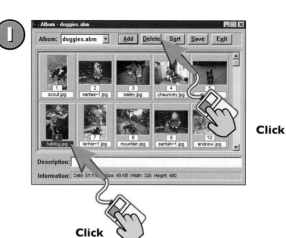

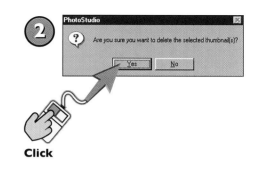

Click

Click

Click

✓ **Deleting Images**
Deleting an image from an album does not delete that image file from your machine's hard drive. In other words, you can access images you've deleted from albums by opening PhotoStudio's **File** menu, choosing **Open**, and selecting the image file from the Open dialog box.

✓ **Selecting Images**
You can easily tell when an image is selected; the image's name and number become highlighted in blue.

① To delete an image, click to select it, and then click the **Delete** button.

② Choose **Yes** to confirm that you want to delete the image from the album.

③ The image is deleted, and subsequent images are renumbered.

Task 5: Rearranging Images Within an Album

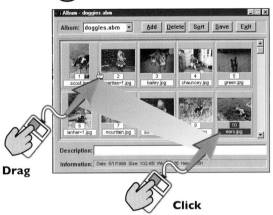

Drag

Click

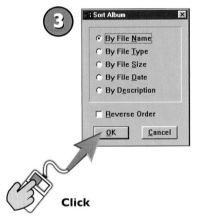

Click

You can easily rearrange the images within an album to make finding the ones you need even easier. For example, using my doggies album, I might want to place all pictures of one dog together, or I might want to sort files by name, type, size, file date, or description.

1 Click the image you want to move, and drag it to the spot where you want it to reside.

2 When you release the mouse button, the image is moved. Repeat until all your images in the album are placed where you want them.

3 To sort images by name, type, size, date, or description, click the **Sort** button, select the type of sort you want, and choose **OK**.

4 The images are sorted (in this case, alphabetically by name).

After you find the image you're looking for in an album, opening it so that you can edit it by using PhotoStudio is easy.

Task 6: Opening an Image from an Album in PhotoStudio

Double-Click

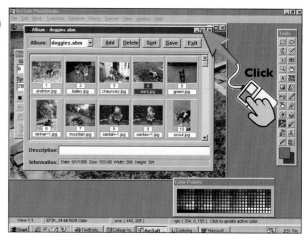

1. Double-click the picture you want to open.

2. The image opens, but is obscured by the Album window. To minimize the Album window, click the **Minimize** button.

3. The Album window is minimized, enabling you to edit the image you opened.

Task 7: Closing an Album

Click

When you've finished working with an album, closing it is easy. This task shows you how.

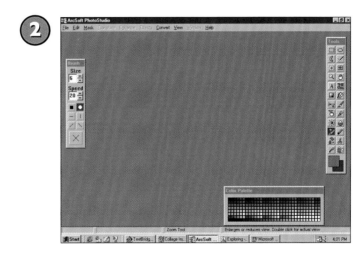

Click the **Exit** button in the Album window.

The album is closed.

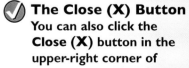

The Close (X) Button
You can also click the **Close (X)** button in the upper-right corner of the Album window to close the album.

End Task

Task 8: Deleting an Album

If you decide you no longer want to store a certain album on your hard drive, you can easily delete it. This task shows you how.

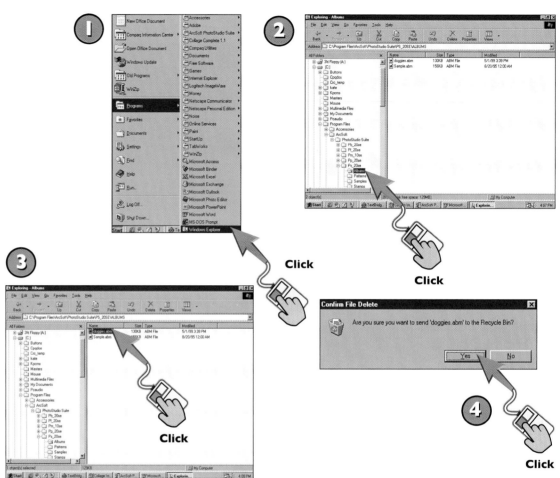

Start Here

Click

Click

Click

Click

Click the **Start** button, choose **Programs**, and select **Windows Explorer**.

In Windows Explorer, navigate to the **C:\Program Files\ArcSoft\PhotoStudio Suite\Ps_20se\Albums** directory.

Click the album you want to delete, and press the **Delete** key on your keyboard.

Choose **Yes** to confirm that you want to delete the album.

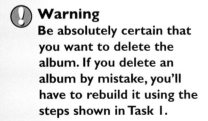

Warning

Be absolutely certain that you want to delete the album. If you delete an album by mistake, you'll have to rebuild it using the steps shown in Task 1.

Next Step

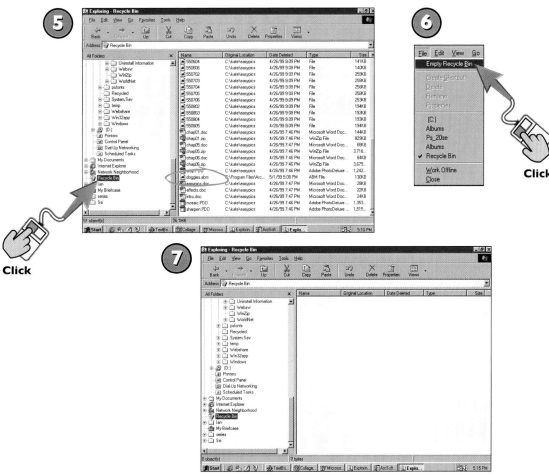

5 In Windows Explorer, scroll to the **Recycle Bin** icon and select it. (Notice the file you deleted.)

6 Open the **File** menu and choose **Empty Recycle Bin**.

7 The Recycle Bin is emptied; the album (and any other files you've deleted) is removed from your hard drive.

✅ **Recycle Bin**
Don't forget that you need to empty the Recycle Bin to completely delete the album from your system.

End
Task

Task 9: Making a Slideshow from an Album

So you just took your digital camera on a trip, and you want to make your friends suffer through a slideshow. No need to dim the lights! Just drag them to your computer, and let the boredom commence.

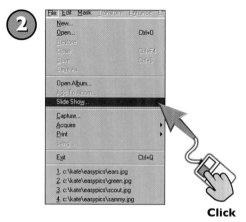

Click

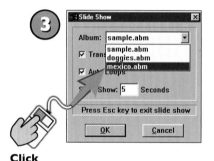

Click

1. Arrange all the photos you want to show in an album.

2. Open PhotoStudio's **File** menu and choose **Slide Show**.

3. Select the album you want to use from the **Album** drop-down list.

4. If you want to view transition effects between each image, leave the **Transition Effect** check box checked.

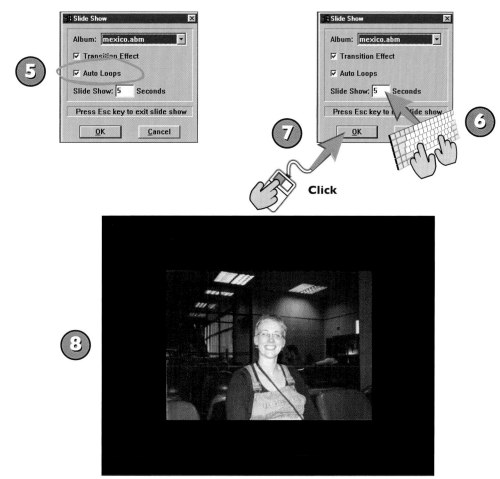

Click

⑤ If you want to repeat the slideshow indefinitely, leave the **Auto Loops** check box checked.

⑥ Specify how long you want each image to be displayed in the **Slide Show** field (5 seconds is the default).

⑦ Choose **OK**.

⑧ The slideshow commences.

✅ **Stop the Show**
To stop the slideshow, press the **Esc** button. (This is especially good to know if you left the **Auto Loops** check box checked.)

✅ **Interrupting Images**
To interrupt the current image and move to the next one, press the **Enter** key on your keyboard.

Projects

So you've figured out all the neat ways you can manipulate your images using your computer—so now what? The possibilities are endless! You can easily paste your pictures on your computer screen as wallpaper; you can add them to letters, spreadsheets, and presentations; you can print greeting cards, brochures, and postcards; you can post them on the Web; you name it.

Tasks

Task 1: Using Your Images as Wallpaper

Tired of your boring old desktop? Why not spice it up with your favorite photo? This task shows you how to turn your favorite digital image into wallpaper for your Windows desktop.

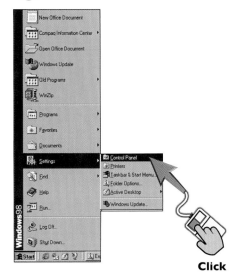

Click

Double-Click

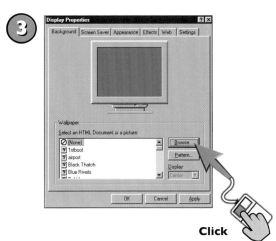

Click

① Open the Control Panel (click the **Start** button, choose **Settings**, and select **Control Panel**).

② In the Control Panel, double-click the **Display** icon.

③ In the **Background** tab of the Display Properties dialog box, click the **Browse** button.

Next Step

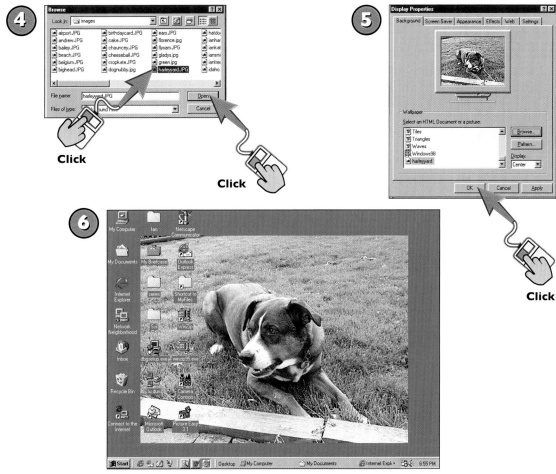

Click

Click

Click

4 Navigate to the spot on your hard drive where your image files are stored. Click the image file you want displayed as wallpaper, and click **Open**.

5 Preview the image in the Display Properties dialog box; click **OK** to close the dialog box and view the wallpaper.

6 The wallpaper is displayed (you might need to minimize any open windows to see it).

Emailing your pictures to your friends is an excellent way to keep everybody up-to-date on your goings-on! This task shows you how to email images as attachments using Microsoft Outlook. If you use a different program, consult its help information about sending attachments.

✓ **File Size**

If you want your mom to be able to print out the image you're sending her, you'll need to send the file in its entirety. If, however, you simply want your mom to see your picture onscreen, reduce the file size to speed up the download time.

First, reduce the file's resolution to 72PPI, which is the highest resolution your screen can reproduce anyhow (see Part 3, Task 8). To compress your file, open PhotoStudio's **File** menu, choose **Save As**, select **JPEG** from the **Save as File Type** drop-down list, and adjust the **Quality** slider (the lower the **Quality** setting, the more the file is compressed).

Task 2: Emailing Images with Microsoft Outlook

Start Here

Click

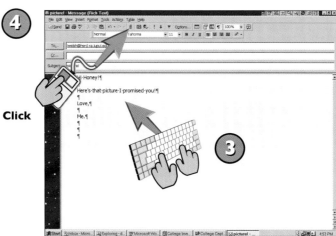

Click

1. After you've compressed your image file, open Outlook Express, go to the Inbox, and click the **New** button.

2. A new message opens. Type the recipient's email address in the **To** field, and type the subject of the message in the **Subject** field.

3. Type your message.

4. To attach a photograph to the message, click the **Add Attachments** button (it's the one with the paper clip).

Next Step

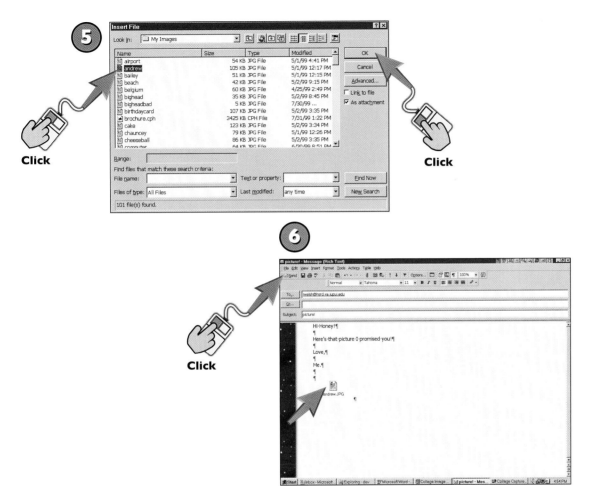

Click

Click

Click

⑤ Locate the file you want to attach, click to select it, and click **OK**.

⑥ The attachment is added to your message. Click the **Send** button.

Embedding Images
Some email programs, including Microsoft Outlook, enable you to embed the image directly into your message—meaning that when the recipient opens the message, she'll be able to immediately see the image. To do this in Outlook, open the **Insert** menu, choose **Picture**, and select **From File**. Locate the image you want to insert, click to select it, and click the **Insert** button.

Inserting pictures in your Word documents is a quick and easy way to spice up an otherwise boring letter or other missive.

Task 3: Adding Pictures to Word Documents

Start Here

Click

Starting Microsoft Word
To start Microsoft Word, click the **Start** button, choose **Programs**, and click **Microsoft Word**.

Importing Pictures
If your scanner is hooked up to your computer, you'll have the option of selecting **From Scanner** in the **Insert, Picture** submenu. Selecting this option enables you to import pictures directly from your scanner for placement on the Word document.

Click

Click

① Click in the Word document where you want to add a picture, and then open the **Insert** menu, choose **Picture**, and select **From File**.

② Navigate to the spot on your hard drive where the picture you want to insert resides, select the picture, and click **Insert**.

Next Step

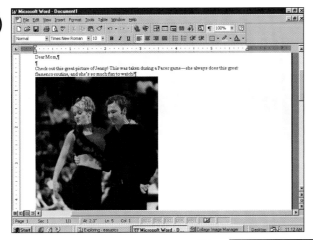

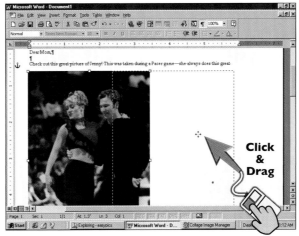

Click & Drag

3 The picture is inserted.

4 To adjust the placement of the picture, click it, and then drag the image where you want it to be.

✅ **Finding the Image**
If you are uncertain where the picture you want to insert is stored on your hard drive, use the search functions located at the bottom of the Insert Picture dialog box.

✅ **Float Over Text**
If you want your text to flow around the image you insert in your document, uncheck the **Float Over Text** check box.

Task 4: Using Pictures to Jazz Up an Excel Spreadsheet

Numbers, numbers, numbers. What could be more boring than a spreadsheet? Well, one way to jazz up your info is to add your favorite digital image to the spreadsheet itself.

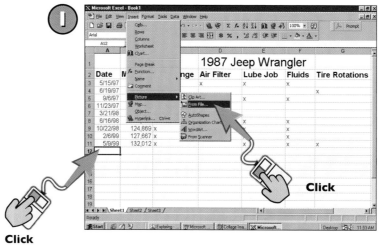

Click

Click

✓ **Starting Microsoft Excel**

To start Microsoft Excel, click the **Start** button, choose **Programs**, and click **Microsoft Excel**.

✓ **The Picture Toolbar**

When you insert your picture, the Picture Toolbar may appear. Use this toolbar to insert additional pictures, to adjust the brightness and contrast, to crop the image, and to add a border, among other things. To remove the toolbar from view, click the **Close (X)** button in its upper-right corner.

If you want to use this toolbar but it is not visible, open the **View** menu, choose **Toolbars**, and select **Picture**.

Click

Click

Click in the Excel spreadsheet where you want to add a picture, and then open the **Insert** menu, choose **Picture**, and select **From File**.

Navigate to the spot on your hard drive where the picture you want to insert resides, select the picture, and click **Insert**.

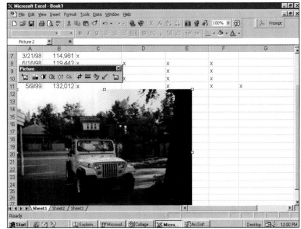

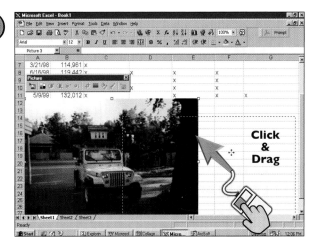

Click & Drag

The picture is inserted.

To adjust the placement of the picture, click it, and then drag the image where you want it to be.

PowerPoint doesn't just have to be for stodgy business presentations. Going to a retirement party? Create a PowerPoint presentation featuring your retiring buddy at work and play! Going to a birthday party? Embarrass the birthday boy with pictures of him at his worst. Rehearsal dinner? Humiliate the bride and groom by showcasing a variety of baby and toddler photos.

Task 5: Creating a PowerPoint Presentation Featuring Your Pictures

Start Here

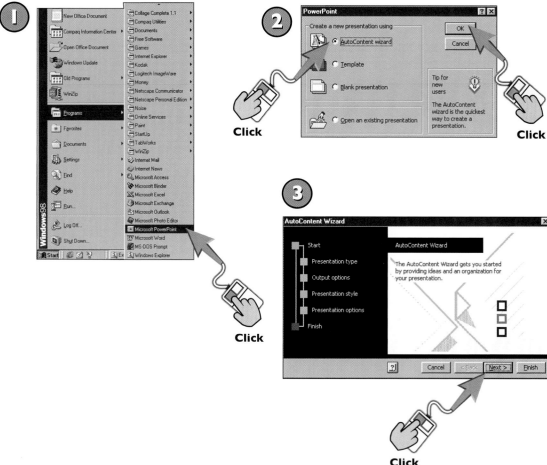

Click

Click

Click

Click

For More on PowerPoint...
This task covers PowerPoint in only a cursory manner. If you want to learn more about how to use this great presentation program, check out Que Publishing's *Easy PowerPoint*.

① To start Microsoft PowerPoint, click the **Start** button, choose **Programs**, and click **Microsoft PowerPoint**.

② Select the **AutoContent Wizard** option button, and click **OK**.

③ Click **Next** in the AutoContent Wizard Start screen.

Next Step

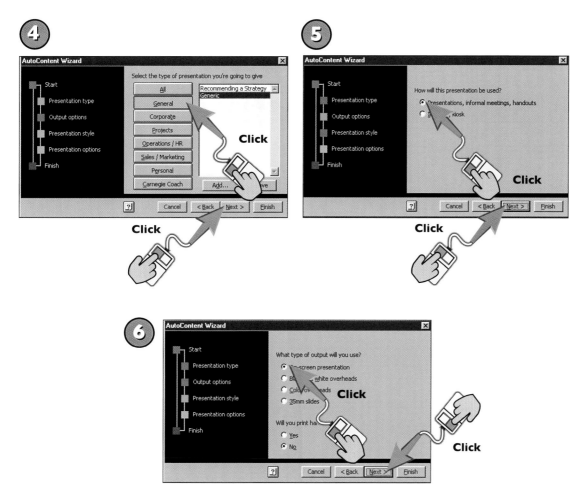

4 Select the presentation type (I've chosen **Generic**), and click **Next**.

5 Specify how the presentation will be used (I've selected the first option button), and click **Next**.

6 Specify the type of output you'll use (**On-screen Presentation** works for me) and whether you'll print handouts, and click **Next**.

Creating a PowerPoint Presentation Featuring Your Pictures Continued

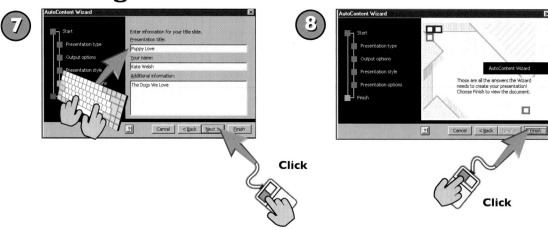

Click

Click

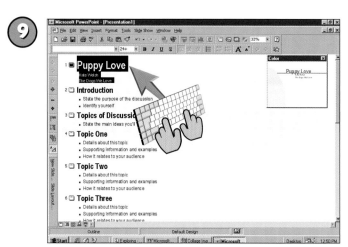

7 Type the name of your presentation and any additional information you want to appear on the title page, and click **Next**.

✓ **Altering the Sample Outline**
Altering the sample outline is a lot like altering text in a word-processing document.

8 Click the **Finish** button.

9 A sample outline for the presentation appears onscreen; to alter it, select each line you want to change, and type over it.

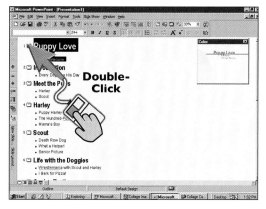

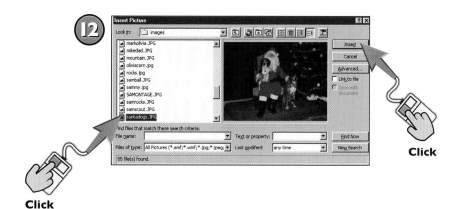

Click

Click

Click

 Double-click the slide icon to the left of the presentation's first slide.

 A full-size version of the slide appears. To add a picture to the slide, open the **Insert** menu, choose **Picture**, and select **From File**.

 Navigate to the spot on your hard drive where the picture you want to insert resides, select the picture, and click **Insert**.

✅ **Inserting Other Items**
In addition to being able to insert your digital pictures, you can also insert a chart, a Microsoft Excel worksheet, a Microsoft Word table, and any number of pieces of clip art.

Next Step

Creating a PowerPoint Presentation Featuring Your Pictures Continued

Click & Drag

Click

Timing Your Transitions

If you want to apply slide transition effects (including sounds) and configure your presentation to automatically advance from slide to slide, open the **Slide Show** menu and choose **Slide Transition**. In the Slide Transition dialog box, select the transition effect you want from the drop-down list (if you don't want to use a transition effect, make sure **No Transition** is selected).

To configure your presentation to automatically advance from slide to slide, click the **Automatically After** check box in the **Advance** section, and enter the number of seconds you want each slide to be visible before being replaced by the next.

Click

  The picture is inserted. To adjust the placement of the picture, click it, and then drag the image where you want it to be.

  Click the **Next Slide** button.

15 Repeat steps 11, 12, 13, and 14 to add images to all the slides in the presentation. When you finish, open the **File** menu and choose **Save As**.

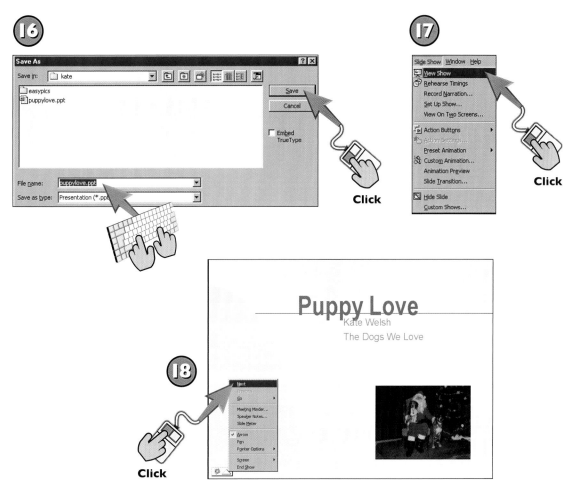

16

17

Click

Click

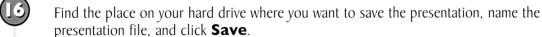

Puppy Love
Kate Welsh
The Dogs We Love

18

Click

16 Find the place on your hard drive where you want to save the presentation, name the presentation file, and click **Save**.

17 Open the **Slide Show** menu and choose **View Show**.

18 The show commences. To move from slide to slide, click the arrow button on the bottom of the screen and choose the desired action from the pop-up menu.

✓ **Adding Sound**
To add sounds to slides in your presentation, open the **Insert** menu, choose **Movies and Sounds,** and select either **Sound from Gallery, Sound from File, Play CD Audio Track,** or **Record Sound** (note: for you to be able to record a sound, your computer must have a microphone).

End Task

Task 6: Putting Your Pictures on the Web

What better way to display your digital pictures than on the Web? That way, friends and family can check out your photos at their leisure. This task shows you how to create a Web site using NetObjects Fusion.

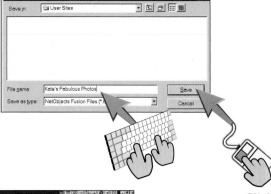

Click

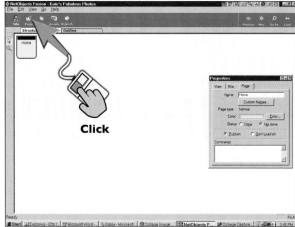

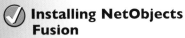

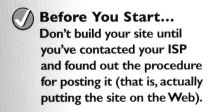

Installing NetObjects Fusion
This book's companion CD comes with a trial version of NetObjects Fusion 4.0; refer to Part 1 for help on installing it.

Before You Start...
Don't build your site until you've contacted your ISP and found out the procedure for posting it (that is, actually putting the site on the Web).

Start NetObjects Fusion. When the Welcome screen appears, click the **Blank Site** option button, and click **OK**.

In the **File Name** field of the New Blank Site dialog box, type a name for your site and click **Save**.

Click the **Page** button in the menu bar.

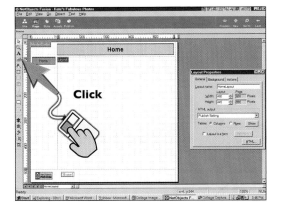

Click

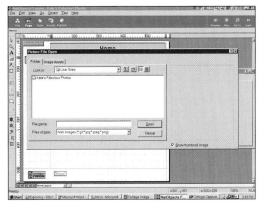

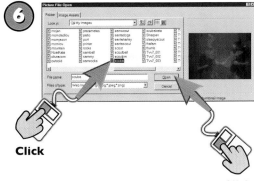

Click

Click

Click

④ To add a photo, click the **Picture** button on the floating tool palette.

⑤ Click and drag to create a box of any size in the layout grid. When you release your mouse button, the Open dialog box appears on your screen.

⑥ Navigate to the folder where the photo you want to add resides, click to select the photo, and click the **Open** button.

Starting NetObjects Fusion
To start NetObjects Fusion, click the **Start** button, choose **Programs**, select **NetObjects**, and click **NetObjects Fusion 4.0 Trial**.

The .nod Extension
NetObject Fusion appends the file extension .nod (Net Object Database) to the site's name.

Want to Know More?
This task covers the bare-bones basics of creating a Web site. If you want to learn more, pick up *Easy Web Pages*.

Moving Objects
You can use the **Arrow** tool in the floating tool palette to move the photo (or any other object) around on the page.

Next Step

Putting Your Pictures on the Web Continued

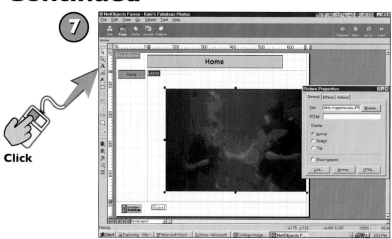

Click

✅ **Changing the Font**
In the Text Properties dialog box, you can select a font, center the text, and more. However, because of HTML language limitations, these options are not as flexible as you might be accustomed to. (If the Text Properties dialog box isn't visible, open the **View** menu and choose **Properties Palette.**)

✅ **Adding More Pages to Your Site**
To add more pages to your site, click the **Site** button in the menu bar. Then, click the **New** button. A new page appears just below the home page; using the Properties dialog box, name this page whatever you like. Add text and images as before.

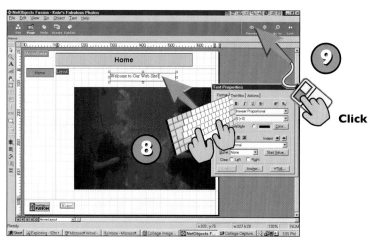

Click

7 The photo appears on the layout grid. To add text, click the **Text** button on the floating tool palette.

8 On the layout grid, click and drag to create a box of any size, and type your text in it.

9 To preview what you have accomplished so far, click the **Preview** button.

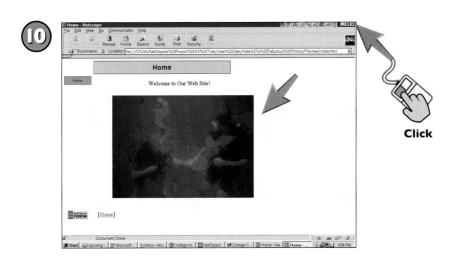

Click

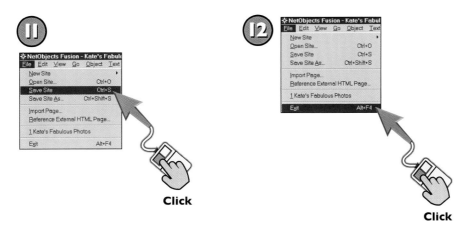

Click

Click

(10) NetObjects converts your site into HTML code and opens your Web browser for you so you can preview the site. Click the **Close (X)** button in the upper-right corner.

(11) To save your page(s), open the **File** menu and select **Save Site**.

(12) To exit NetObjects, open the **File** menu and select **Exit**.

Posting Your Site
Just because you've created your site in **NetObjects Fusion** doesn't mean your friends and family can immediately visit it. Before that can happen, your page must be posted to the Web. Check with your Internet service provider (ISP) for information on posting your site.

Task 7: Making Postcards with Your Images

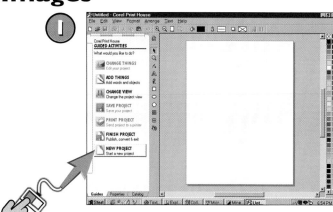

If you're a fan of postcards, you'll love **Print House Magic.** It enables you to make postcards out of your own images! This task shows you how.

Click

Click

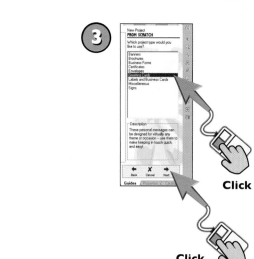

Click

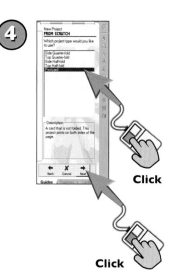

Click

Click

Click

✓ **Starting Print House Magic**
You start Print House Magic just like you do any other program in Windows: from the **Start** menu. Click **Start,** choose **Programs,** select **Corel Print House Magic 4 Premium,** and click **Corel Print House 4.**

1 In Corel Print House Magic, click the **New Project** button.

2 Click **From Scratch** to create a postcard of your own design.

3 Click the **Greeting Cards** entry in the list, and click **Next.**

4 Select the **Postcard** option, and click **Next.**

Next Step ▶

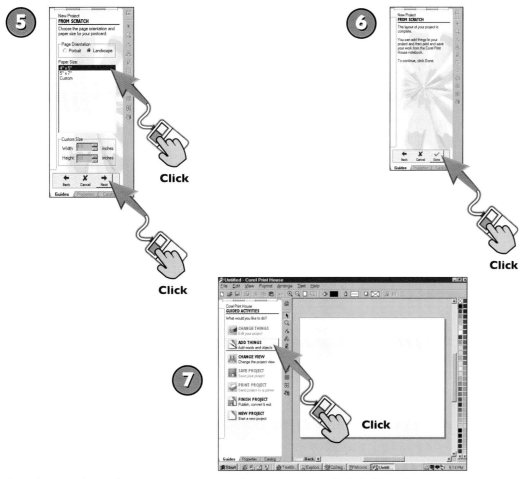

5 Specify your desired page orientation and paper size, and click **Next**.

6 Click **Done**.

7 To add an image to the front of your postcard, click **Add Things**.

Adding Text
If you want to add text to the front of your postcard, select **Text** from the same menu where you select **Import Item**, then click the location where you want to add text and begin typing. Change the font by clicking **Change Font** in the left pane and selecting the font you want.

Saving Your Project
If you want to save your postcard for later use, click **Save Project** in the **Guides** tab. In the **Save File** dialog box, navigate to the spot where you want to save the card, type a name for it, and click **Save**.

Making Postcards with Your Images Continued

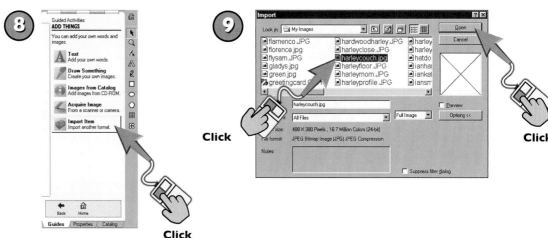

Moving Objects
To move an image or text, simply click and drag it where you want it to be.

Resizing Objects
To make an image or text larger or smaller, simply click on one of the selection handles and drag until the object is the size you want. To proportionally resize an object (that is, to increase or decrease both the height and the width at the same time), click and drag one of the corner handles.

⑧ Click **Import Item** to add an image stored on your hard drive.

⑨ The Import dialog box appears; select the image you want to add, and click **Open**.

⑩ The image is added to the postcard. Resize and move it as needed.

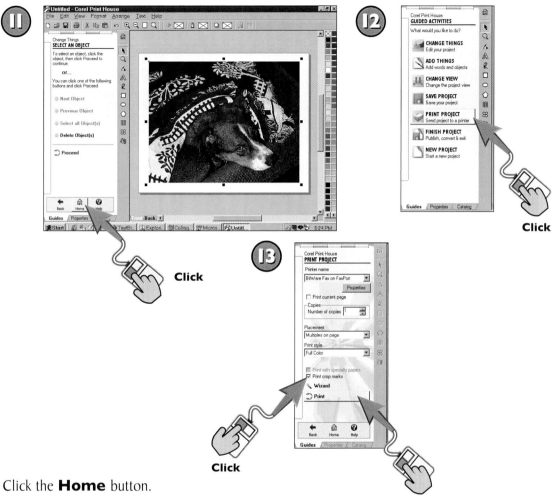

Click

Click

Click

Click

Print Options
Print House Magic's print options are pretty standard: you specify the printer you want to use, whether you want to print only the current page (not applicable here), the number of copies you want to print, whether you want to print multiple copies of your project on each sheet of paper, and whether you want it to print full color. You can also specify whether you want the printer to print crop marks, which can make it easier for you to know where to cut if needed.

Paper
You'll want to use a fairly heavy-stock paper when printing postcards; also, make sure the paper you select is relatively glossy so that your image doesn't look too matte.

11 Click the **Home** button.

12 Click **Print Project**.

13 Set your print options (note that I've selected the **Print Crop Marks** option so that I'll know where to cut to create the postcard) and click **Print**.

End Task

Task 8: Making Greeting Cards

Imagine the money you'll save this year when you make your own holiday cards, using your own images and expressing your own message! This task shows you how.

✓ **Insert the CD!**
Make sure that this book's companion CD has been inserted into your CD-ROM drive before you start this task. You'll need to use special background templates that are stored there.

✓ **Special Paper?**
If you've purchased special paper for printing greeting cards, such as the kind made by Kodak, Avery, or PaperDirect, you should click **From Sample** instead of **From Scratch** in step 2. Then, select the paper manufacturer and the precise type of paper you bought. Click **Done**, and proceed as normal starting with step 7.

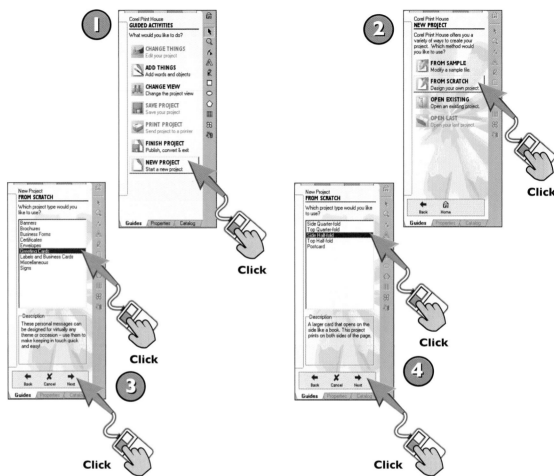

Start Here

Click · Click · Click · Click · Click · Click

1. In Corel Print House Magic, click the **New Project** button (see the tip in Task 7, "Making Postcards with Your Images," if you need help starting this program).

2. Click **From Scratch** to create a greeting card of your own design.

3. Click the **Greeting Cards** entry in the list, and click **Next**.

4. Specify which type of card you want. I've chosen **Side Half-fold** to create a larger card that opens like a book. Click **Next**.

Next Step

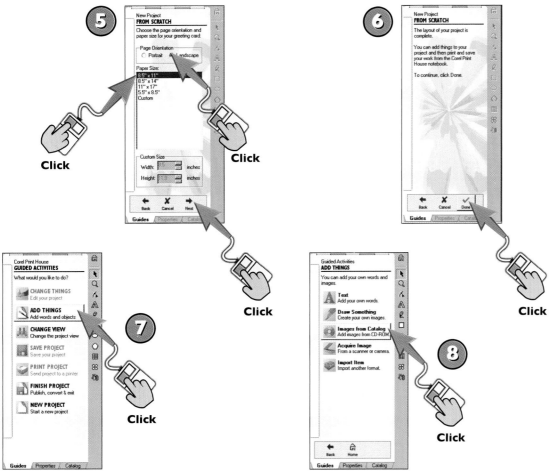

5. To make a traditional card that opens like a book, select the **Landscape** option button. Select the paper size you plan to use, and click **Next**.

6. Click the **Done** button.

7. To add a background image to your card, click the **Add Things** button.

8. Click the **Images from Catalog** option to access (among other things) predesigned card templates.

Next Step

Making Greeting Cards Continued

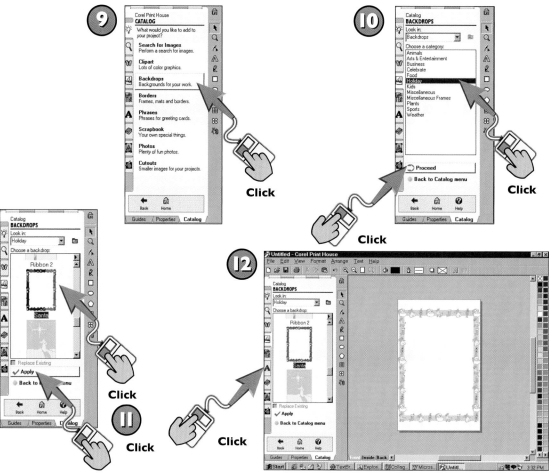

Click

Click

Click

Click

Click

Click

⑨ Click the **Backdrops** option.

⑩ Select a category (because I'm making a holiday card, I've chosen **Holiday**), and click **Proceed**.

⑪ Scroll through the available backdrops until you find one that suits your needs. Click it, and then click **Apply**.

⑫ The backdrop you selected is applied to the card. To add text, click the **Phrases** button (the one with an "A" on it) on the toolbar along the left side of the screen.

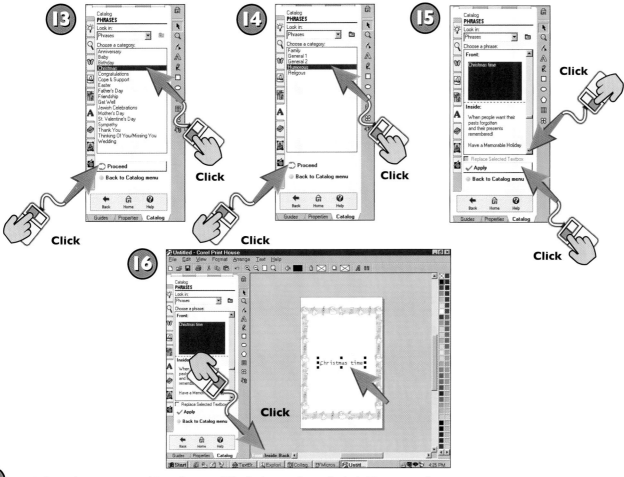

13 Select the occasion (I've chosen **Christmas**), and click **Proceed**.

14 Select the type of phrase you're looking for (I've chosen **Humorous**), and click **Proceed**.

15 Scroll until you find a phrase that you like, and then click the **Apply** button.

16 The phrase you selected is applied to the front of the card. Click the **Inside** tab.

Making Greeting Cards Continued

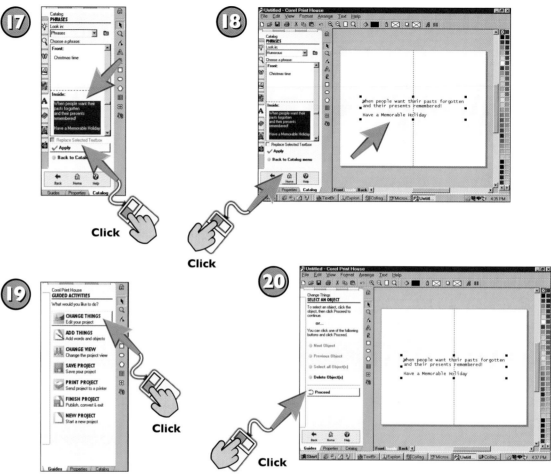

Click

Click

Click

Click

17 In the **Choose a Phrase** area on the left side of the screen, select the phrase under **Inside** and click **Apply**.

18 The selected text is added to the inside of the card. Click the **Home** button.

19 Click **Change Things**.

20 With the text still selected, click **Proceed**.

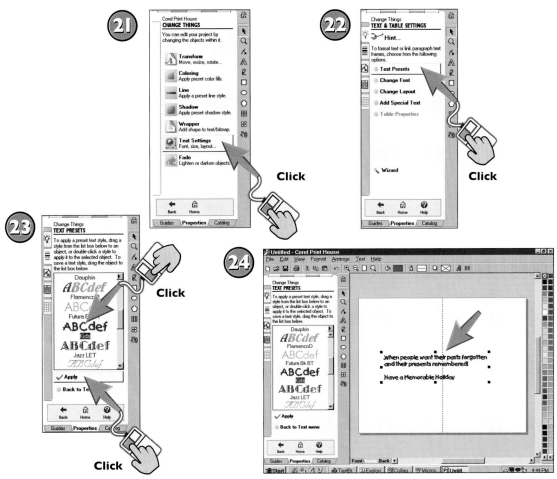

Click

Click

Click

Click

21 Click **Text Settings**.

22 Click **Text Presets** to choose from among several preset text styles.

23 Select the preset text style that you like, and click **Apply**.

24 The style you chose is applied to the selected text.

✓ **Undo**
If you make a mistake, open the **Edit** menu and choose **Undo**.

✓ **You Don't Have to Use the Presets...**
If you don't like any of the preset text styles, you can set your own font. Simply click **Change Font** instead of **Text Presets** in step 22.

Making Greeting Cards Continued

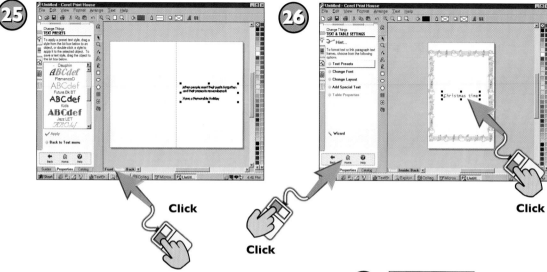

Click

Click

Click

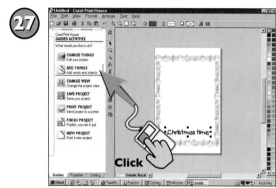

Click

Click

✓ **Moving Objects**
To move the image or text, simply click and drag it where you want it to be.

✓ **Resizing Objects**
To make the image or text larger or smaller, click one of the selection handles and drag until the object is the size you want. To proportionally resize an object (that is, to increase or decrease both the height and the width at the same time), click and drag one of the corner handles.

✓ **Paper**
You'll want to use a fairly heavy-stock paper when printing greeting cards; also, make sure the paper you select is relatively glossy so that your image doesn't look too matte.

25) Move and resize the text as needed, and then click the **Front** tab.

26) Click the text on the front of the card to select it, and then repeat steps 22–24. Move and resize the text as needed, and then click the **Home** button.

27) Click **Add Things** to add an image to the front of the card.

28) Click **Import Item** to add an image stored on your hard drive.

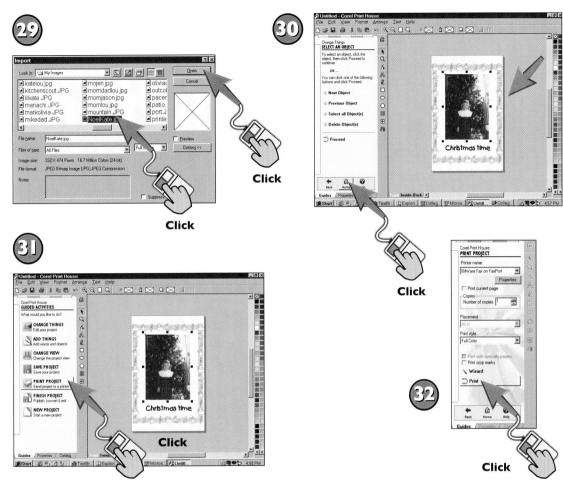

Click

Click

Click

Click

Click

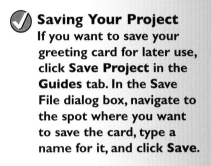

✓ Saving Your Project
If you want to save your greeting card for later use, click **Save Project** in the **Guides** tab. In the Save File dialog box, navigate to the spot where you want to save the card, type a name for it, and click **Save**.

✓ Special Paper?
If you elected to create your greeting card using special paper (refer to the tip on the first page of this task), notice that the **Print with Specialty Papers** check box is checked in the printer options area. (This option is available only when you start your project using a specialty papers sample.) Before you print a project on specialty paper, print a test page to verify whether the front or the back prints first, and to verify paper orientation.

(29) The Import dialog box appears; select the image you want to add, and click **Open**.

(30) The image appears on the card (possibly obscuring the text you added earlier). Move and resize the image and text as needed, and then click the **Home** button.

(31) Click **Print Project** to send the card to the printer.

(32) Set your print options, and click **Print**.

End Task

Task 9: Making a Calendar

Why buy a calendar when you can make your own—complete with all your favorite pictures?

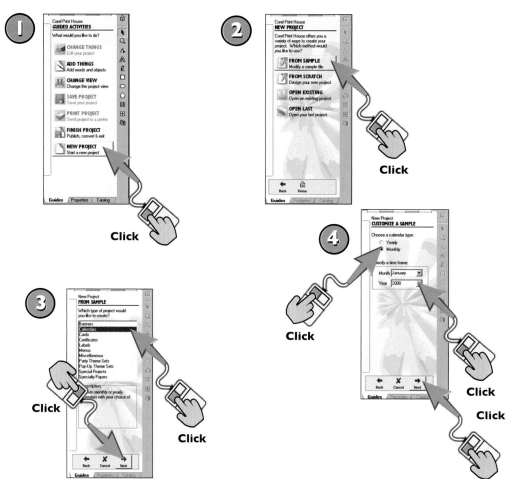

1. In Corel Print House Magic, click the **New Project** button (refer to the tip in Task 7 if you need help starting this program).

Insert the CD!
Make sure that this book's companion CD has been inserted into your CD-ROM drive before you start this task.

2. Click **From Sample**.

3. Click **Calendars** to select it, and then click **Next**.

4. Select the type of calendar you want (**Yearly** or **Monthly**), and then choose the month and year from the drop-down list. Click **Next**.

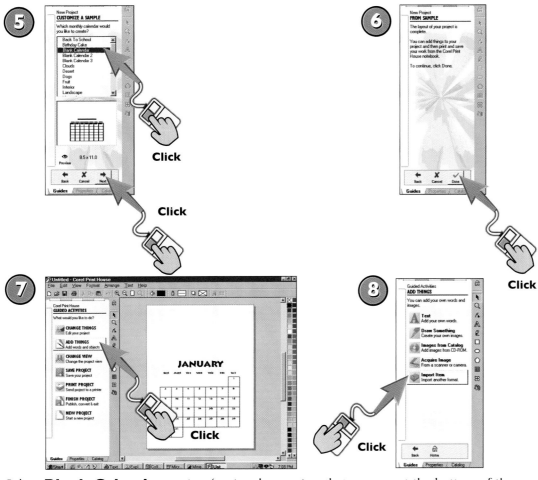

5 Select **Blank Calendar** option (notice the preview that appears at the bottom of the panel) and click **Next**.

6 Click **Done**.

7 The calendar template appears in the right pane; click **Add Things**.

8 Click **Import Item**.

Making a Calendar Continued

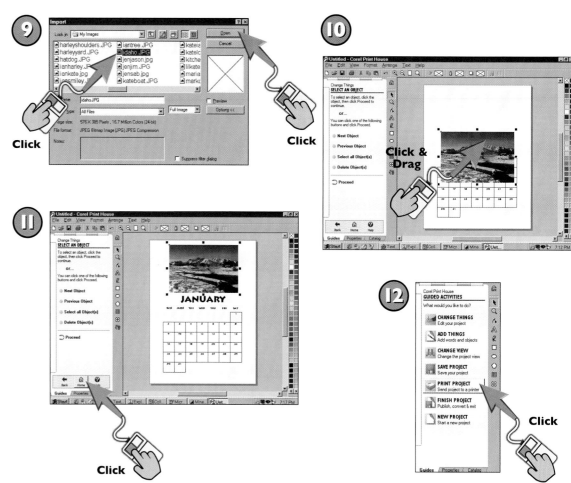

Click

Click

Click & Drag

Click

Click

Click

⑨ The Import dialog box appears; select the image you want to add to the calendar, and click **Open**.

⑩ The image appears on the calendar. Move and resize it as needed.

⑪ Click the **Home** button.

⑫ Click **Print Project**.

Next Step

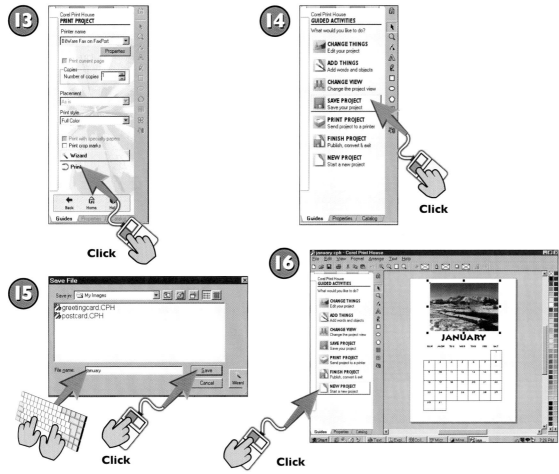

Click

Click

Click

Click

13 Set your print options, and click **Print**.

14 Click **Save Project**.

15 Type a name for the file in the Save File dialog box (I've typed **January**), and click **Save**.

16 Repeat steps 1–15 for each month you want to add to your calendar.

You can use specialty papers for any number of projects, including printing stickers of your photos. This task shows you how to make stickers using Kodak specialty papers; visit www.kodak.com to order sticker paper online.

Task 10: Creating Stickers of Your Photos Using Kodak Specialty Papers

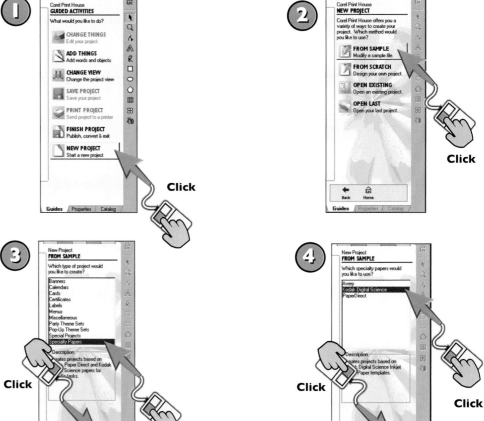

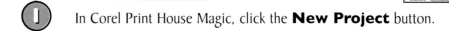

✓ **Insert the CD!**
Make sure that this book's companion CD has been inserted into your CD-ROM drive before you start this task.

In Corel Print House Magic, click the **New Project** button.

Click **From Sample**.

Select **Specialty Papers**, and click **Next**.

Select **Kodak Digital Science**, and click **Next**.

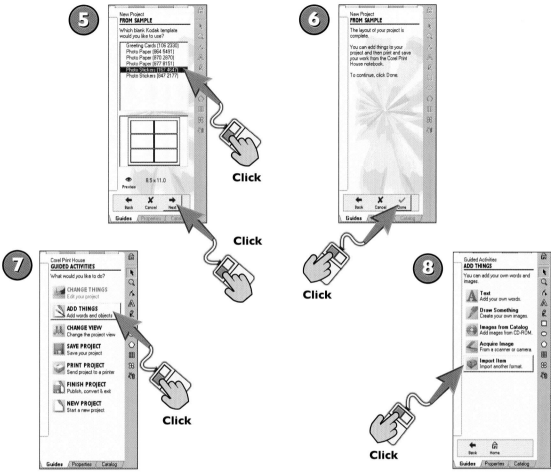

5 Select the type of photo stickers you have—I've selected **Photo Stickers (167 4647)**. Click **Next**.

6 Click **Done**.

7 Click **Add Things**.

8 Click **Import Item**.

Creating Stickers of Your Photos Using Kodak Specialty Papers Continued

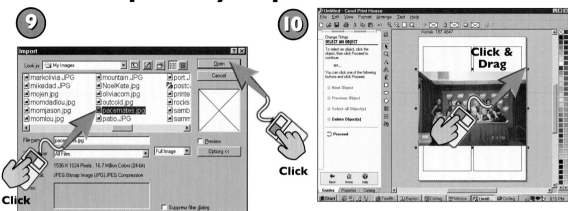

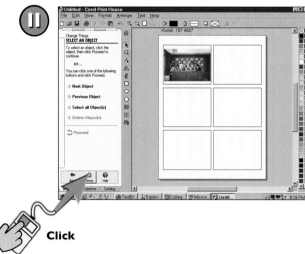

9 Select the first image you want to turn into a sticker, and click **Open**.

10 The image is added. Resize and move it as needed.

11 Click **Home**.

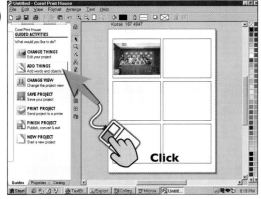

Click

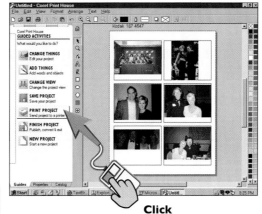

Click

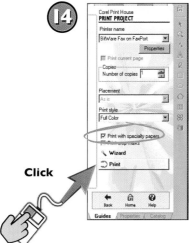

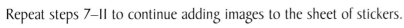

Click

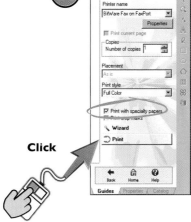

12 Repeat steps 7–11 to continue adding images to the sheet of stickers.

13 Click **Print Project**.

14 Set your print options (notice that **Print with Specialty Papers** is already checked), and click **Print**.

✅ **Saving Your Project**
If you want to save your stickers for later use, click **Save Project** in the **Guides** tab. In the **Save File** dialog box, navigate to the spot where you want to save the card, type a name for it, and click **Save**.

End
Task

Task 11: Creating a Brochure Using PaperDirect Specialty Papers

If you own a small business, you know how expensive it can be to have brochures designed and printed by someone else. With Print House Magic, you can design and print your own! This task shows you how to create a brochure using PaperDirect specialty papers; you'll need to visit www.paperdirect.com to order brochure paper before you proceed with this task.

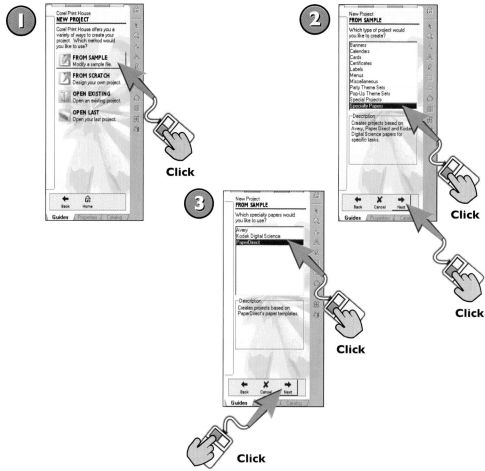

Click

Click

Click

Click

Click

1   Click **From Sample**.

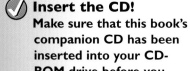

Insert the CD!
Make sure that this book's companion CD has been inserted into your CD-ROM drive before you start this task.

2   Select **Specialty Papers**, and click **Next**.

3   Select **PaperDirect**, and click **Next**.

Next
Step

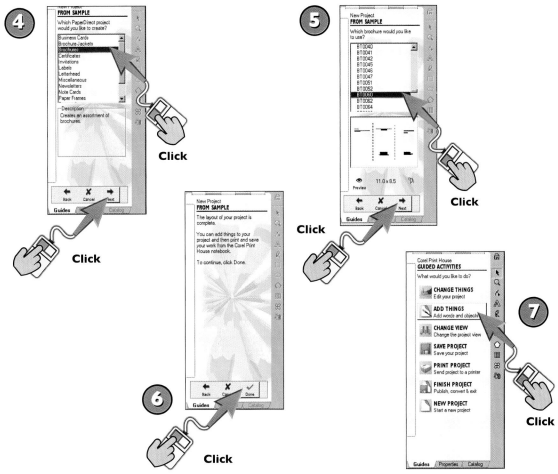

Click

Click

Click

Click

Click

Click

4. Select the **Brochures** option, and click **Next**.

5. Select the brochure you want to use (click a few and check the preview to decide which one you want). Click **Next**.

6. Click **Done**.

7. A template for your brochure appears; click **Add Things**.

Creating a Brochure Using PaperDirect Specialty Papers Continued

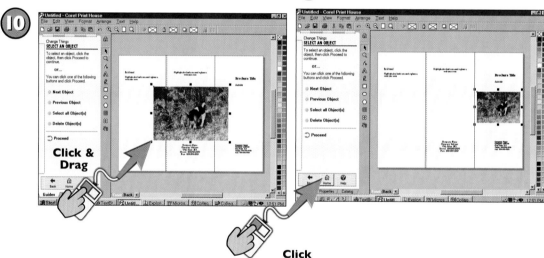

⑧ Click **Import Item** to add an image saved on your hard drive.

⑨ Select the image you want to add to the brochure and click **Open**.

⑩ The image is added. Resize and move it as needed.

⑪ Click the **Home** button. Repeat steps 7–11 to add more images to the front of your brochure.

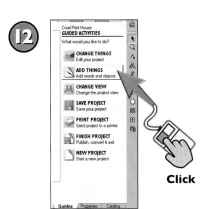

Click

Click

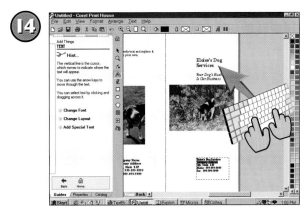

12 After you've added the images you want to the front of your brochure, click **Add Things** to begin adding text.

13 Click **Text**.

14 Select the dummy text, and type over it with the text you want to add to your brochure. Do this for all dummy text on the front of the brochure.

Next Step

✅ **Using the Zoom Tools**
To get a better look at the text areas, use the Zoom tools on the toolbar at the top of the screen (the **Zoom In** button has a magnifying glass with a plus sign [+] on it; the **Zoom Out** button has a magnifying glass with a minus sign [–] on it). Use the scrollbars to navigate the brochure after you've zoomed in on it.

✅ **Changing the Font**
If you don't like the font that is automatically applied to the text on your brochure, change it by clicking the **Change Font** option in the left panel.

Creating a Brochure Using PaperDirect Specialty Papers Continued

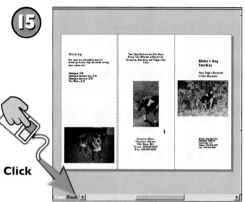

Click

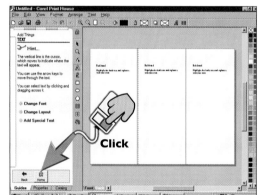

Click

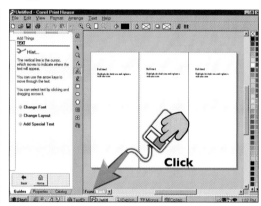

Click

✓ **Changing Things**
If you want to change the position, color, font, and so on of a certain element, click the element, click the **Home** button, and then choose **Change Things.** You'll see a list of options; select the one that suits your needs.

15 After you've finished with the front of the brochure, click the **Back** tab.

16 Click the **Home** button.

17 Repeat steps 8–16 to add images and text to the back of the brochure. When you're finished, click the **Front** tab.

Next
Step ▶

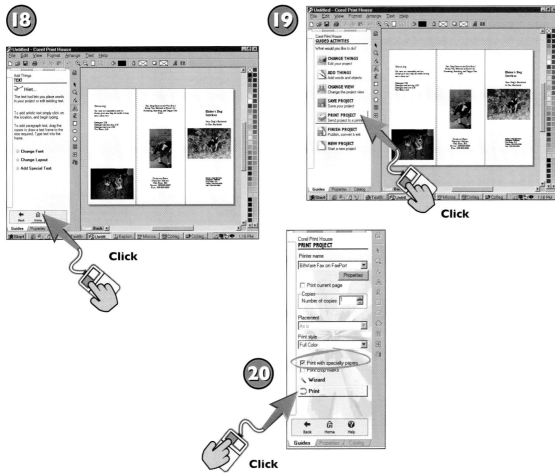

18 Click **Home**.

19 Click **Print Project**.

20 Set your print options (notice that **Print with Specialty Papers** is already checked), and click **Print**.

8-bit image   8-bit images display 256 colors, which is fairly standard when working with digital images that you don't plan to print.

24-bit True Color   Systems that display 24-bit True Color display 16,000,000 colors—about as many colors as can be seen by the human eye.

active color   The active color is the color currently selected from the Color palette. The active color is the color that will be applied to your image if you use any of the painting or drawing tools. You can tell which color is the active color by looking at the top-most swatch at the bottom of the Tools palette.

active image   The active image is the image you're currently working on. When an image is the active image, the title bar of its window is darker than the title bars of other open images on the PhotoStudio desktop.

Airbrush tool   Simulates the effect of an airbrush, slowly adding layers of the current active color on top of areas where you click and drag.

alternative color   The alternative color is the one visible in the bottom-most swatch at the bottom of the Tools palette. The alternative color is applied when certain tools in the Tools palette are used (such as the Gradient tool).

Area Move tool   Moves both a mask and the pixels that lie within its boundaries. To use it, click in the current mask and drag the masked area to its new location.

aspect ratio   This term refers to the ratio of an image's height to its width.

bit   The smallest unit of storage on a computer.

bit depth   The amount of information each pixel in an image contains.

BMP   Abbreviation for bitmap. A file format for color and grayscale images (used by Microsoft Windows).

Brighten/Darken tool
Brightens or darkens the area in your image where you click and drag the mouse.

brightness   This term refers to how much black or white is mixed with a color.

Brush palette   You use the Brush palette to specify the shape, size, and drawing speed of the brush. Settings in this palette apply to the Airbrush, Pen, Paintbrush, Smudge, Brighten/Darken, Smooth/Sharpen, and Revert tools.

Bucket Fill tool   Selects an area based on color similarity and adds the active color to it.

channel   One component of a color model. For example, for the RGB color model, the channels are red, green, and blue.

Clone tool   Duplicates one part of your image in another part of the image.

CMYK   A standard color model for printing full-color images and documents. The channels in this color system are cyan, magenta, yellow, and black.

color correction   When you color-correct an image, you adjust the channels of all or part of an image to get a truer representation.

color depth   This term is used to describe the amount of memory available to specify the color of one pixel in an image (as in 24-bit color). The more bits you can use to specify this color, the more colors you have available to you overall—meaning that the odds of your image matching real life increase.

color mapping   Color mapping is when you remap current color intensities to the intensities that you want by adjusting a curve on a "map"—a simple two-dimensional graph.

color model   A system for describing colors. The standard color models are RGB (describes colors in terms of their quantities of red, green, and blue), HSV (specifies a color in terms of its hue, saturation or intensity, and brightness), and CMYK (describes colors in terms of their percentages of cyan, magenta, yellow, and black).

Color palette   In PhotoStudio, a palette containing a broad assortment of colors for quick color selection.

color scheme   See color model.

color swatch   Squares on the Tools palette that display both the active color and the alternative colors.

color value   A number that describes a certain color. In the RGB color model, for example, each color has a color value that consists of three numbers ranging from 0 to 255 (each number represents the prominence of red, green, and blue in the given color). So, for example, the color value for pure red is 255,0,0 (all red, no blue, no green).

compression   Files containing images are typically compressed—otherwise, they would be so large that cameras could store only a few images at any given time (not to mention the fact that images would take forever to download). There are two forms of compression: *lossy* and *lossless*.

contrast   The difference between bright and dark colors in your image. When you increase an image's contrast, you increase this difference; bright colors become brighter and dark ones become darker.

crop   The process of omitting all but the selected area from an image.

Crop tool   When you click the Crop button, the selected part of your image is copied and poured into a new image window (the original image is left untouched).

dithering   When an image does not have enough resolution to accurately represent certain colors, those colors are simulated through dithering. When an image is dithered, dots of other colors are placed close together so that they average out to appear like the intended color. This gives the image a rough, speckled appearance.

DPI   Dots per inch. A higher DPI means a higher-quality image or printout. *See also* resolution.

Ellipse Select tool   Use this tool to select elliptical or oval-shaped portions of your image.

Eyedropper tool   Makes the active color the same as the color of the point in the image on which you click.

file type   The format in which a file is stored. You can save graphics files using a number of different file types, including BMP, JPEG (recommended for digital photographs), PCX, TGA, and TIFF.

filter   A visual effect that can be applied to an image.

floating selection   An area in an image that can be deleted or moved without affecting the image on which it sits.

Freehand Select tool   Use this tool to select irregularly shaped areas in your image.

gamut   The range of colors that can be reproduced by any device.

GIF   A standard file format for color and grayscale images. GIF files can contain up to eight bits of color information per pixel.

Grabber tool   Use the Grabber tool to adjust the position of your image in the image window.

gradient   A transition from one color to another.

Gradient Fill tool   Use this tool to fill the current mask (or, if there is no mask, the entire image) with a gradient from the alternative color to the active color.

highlights   The brightest parts of an image.

histogram   A line chart showing the color distributions of an image.

HSV   A color model that defines colors in terms of hue, saturation, and brightness.

hue   The color channel in HSV that defines what part of the spectrum a color belongs to.

image data type   Describes an image's pixel and color information. The image data type is usually composed of the bit depth (for example, 24-bit), and the color model (RGB, for instance).

image editor   A piece of software (such as PhotoStudio) that enables you to edit and otherwise manipulate digital images.

indexed-color image   An image that has been reduced to 16 or 256 colors. When an image is reduced to 16 or 256 colors, the image editor (in your case, PhotoStudio) determines which 16 or 256 colors best represent the image. Each pixel in the image that contains a color not in the chosen set of colors is *indexed* to the closest color in the set (also, sometimes colors not in the set are approximated by dithering).

invert   To reverse the colors of an image to their opposites (like creating a photographic negative).

JPEG   A file format that encodes color or grayscale images in a compressed form.

lossless compression   When you uncompress an image that was compressed using lossless compression, the quality of the uncompressed image matches that of the original image. Although this type of compression sounds ideal, it typically doesn't compress files enough to make much of a difference.

lossy compression   The type of compression used by most digital cameras. Although using lossy compression does degrade images, this type of compression enables much smaller files than does lossless; additionally, the degradation of images is typically not noticeable (except in the case of an enlarged print of the image). JPEG is an example of a file format that uses lossy compression.

LZW compression   A type of lossless compression used to reduce the size of image files.

Magic Wand Select tool Use this tool to select an area of your image based on color similarity. For example, if you want to select the green grass in your yard but not the purple crocuses, you can use the Magic Wand Select tool to select the grass without selecting the flowers.

mask A mask, which you create by using the selection tools (and which is marked on your screen by a moving dotted line), isolates the editing area, preventing unmasked areas from being altered. Masks can also be used to designate areas you want to copy or cut.

Mask Move tool This tool enables you to move a mask to a different part of your image without altering the image itself.

midtones The parts of an image that are of middling brightness (or the colors of those parts).

noise Random interference and degradation in an image (like snow on a television).

opacity The opposite of *transparency*. Something is 100% opaque when you can't see through it at all.

Paintbrush tool Use this tool to apply a layer of the active color to the area where you click and drag.

palettes Windows on the PhotoStudio screen that contain tools (the Tools palette), controls (the Brush palette), and color selections (the Color palette).

PCD A file format designed by Eastman Kodak for its PhotoCD system.

PCX A file format designed by ZSoft Corporation for PC-based painting programs.

Pen tool This tool applies the active color like a marker or felt-tip pen.

pixel Basically a dot, a *pixel* is the smallest element of a digital image.

posterize To decrease the quantity of an image's color values. This creates an impressionistic effect.

rasterization The process of converting an image into a bitmap form (so that it can be printed by an inkjet or laser printer).

Rectangle Select tool Use this tool to select rectangular portions of your image.

resample When you resample an image, you alter its dimensions and resolution.

resolution The pixel density of an image. Higher-resolution images have greater density and better appearance.

Revert tool This tool is similar to an eraser, enabling you to blend the changes you've made to the masked area with the underlying image area.

RGB A color model based on three channels: red, green, and blue.

saturation One of three channels in the HSV color model, saturation measures how pure a color is.

scanner A hardware device that "reads" photographs, creating a digital image copy of the original.

selected area The selected area is the part of an image that lies within a mask.

shadows   The darkest areas of an image.

Smooth/Sharpen tool
Depending on whether this tool is set to Smooth or Sharpen, this tool enables you to smooth rough edges and harsh transitions, and to sharpen areas that seem fuzzy.

Smudge tool   The Smudge tool simulates a finger smearing your image.

Stamp tool   Using the Stamp tool, you can click your image to place a pre-defined shape on it. Not only can you stamp shapes provided by PhotoStudio, but you can also create your own stamp shapes.

Text tool   Using the Text tool, you can add text to any part of your image.

TGA   Sometimes referred to as "Targa," TGA is a file format for color and grayscale raster images.

threshold   A numeric limit (defined by the user) based on color values that divides all the colors in an image into two groups: one containing colors with values equal to or below the threshold, and another containing colors with values above the threshold.

thumbnail   A small version of an image; thumbnail images are especially useful in Web pages, because their files are typically smaller than full-size images, meaning that they don't take as long to download.

TIFF   A file format that stores color and grayscale images; this format is often used to transfer images between different applications and different types of computers.

Tools palette   Contains tools for selecting, viewing, drawing, painting, retouching, and editing images (also contains controls for choosing the active and alternative colors).

Transform tool   Use this tool to resize, rotate, skew, and distort the current selection.

transparency   The extent to which you can see through one image element (such as paint applied by the Paintbrush tool) to the original image underneath it.

Trash Can tool   Click the Trash Can button in PhotoStudio to remove the current mask and all changes that have been made in it.

TWAIN   Stands for "Technology Without an Interesting Name." A standard for image input from scanners, digital cameras, video grabbers, and the like. Programs that support TWAIN (such as PhotoStudio) can receive image input from any TWAIN-compatible device (as long as the system's hardware and software have been set up or configured correctly).

zoom   To enlarge (zoom in) or reduce (zoom out) the size of the current image view.

Zoom tool   Selecting the Zoom tool and then clicking the active image magnifies your view of the image.

Shooting Good Pictures

You can avoid having to sharpen, crop, edit, or airbrush your images—not to mention adjusting their brightness, contrast, hue, saturation, or tone—by taking good pictures in the first place. Some common problems include

- Bad lighting

- Blurred images

- Poor composition

Use the tips in this appendix to avoid these types of problems, and improve your photos!

Bad Lighting

Bad lighting is probably the culprit if your image lacks brightness, contrast, or the proper tone. You can compensate for a lot of lighting woes, including backlight and low-light conditions (and even the harsh effects of sunlight), by using a flash. Your camera may have an automatic flash, in which case it flashes whenever it thinks it needs to. If not, you'll have to set it manually; see your camera's documentation for more information.

Blurred Images

Blurred images can be caused by several things, many of which are easy to correct.

Keep It Steady!

Seems obvious, but the greatest factor in lousy photos is an unsteady hand. If your pictures are often blurry, this may be the culprit. To avoid this problem, concentrate on keeping your arms close to your side and, if possible, brace yourself against a building, fence, or other solid object. Also, some say that holding your breath while you press the shutter button can prevent the shakes. Finally, if you're really serious about taking good pictures, consider using a tripod.

Back Off

Lots of cameras have a minimum focusing distance, meaning that you have to be a certain distance from your subject for your image not to be blurred. (Check your camera's documentation to determine what this distance is.)

Shutter Speed

Your shutter speed can greatly affect the sharpness of your images. The rule of thumb to follow: The faster your subject is moving, the faster your shutter speed should be (but unless you're using a tripod, you should always avoid particularly slow speeds—even if your subject is completely still).

Poor Composition

If you take a few moments to consider the composition of a scene before you snap your picture, you'll find that your photos become more eye-catching and require less manipulation with image-editing software.

Parallax

With some cameras, the scene you see through the viewfinder isn't necessarily the image you'll get when you finally take the picture—the outcome being that you guillotine the tops of your subjects' heads, or end up with your thumb in the final print. This is because the viewfinder is separate from the lens, and offers only an approximation of the scene (called *parallax*). Avoiding this problem is a matter of practicing with your camera to get a feel for its limitations; also, be sure to read your camera's manual to see what it recommends.

Eyesores

Sometimes, when you're setting up a shot, it's hard to notice when a telephone pole seems to be erupting from the head of your mother-in-law or when your dad appears to have a plant as hair. Nonetheless, if you train yourself to look for these types of eyesores, you'll witness a definite improvement in your photos (and save time by not having to edit those eyesores from your image using image-editing software).

Vertical Versus Horizontal

Wait! Before you press that shutter button, consider whether the scene you're about to capture will look best as a horizontal picture or a vertical one.

Off Center

Instead of putting your subject smack in the middle of the frame, try putting them to one side or another to capture more of the scene.

Eye Level

Shoot your subject at eye level. If you're taking a picture of a turtle, lie on the ground for the shot. If you're taking a picture of Shaquille O'Neal, stand on a chair.

Index

Symbols

3D Grid filter, 111

A

Acquire command (File menu), 38, 56
acquiring images
    from digital cameras (PhotoStudio), 56-57
    scanners, 58-59
acquisition software, 56-59
active color, 69
Add Attachments button, 154-155
Add Frame command (Edit menu), 100
Add Printer Wizard, 14-15
Add to Album dialog box, 139-141
Add/Remove Programs icon (Control Panel), 10
adding
    images
        to brochures, 192-195
        to calendars, 182-185
        to greeting cards, 175-181
        to postcards, 170-173
        to Word documents, 156-157
    pictures
        to PowerPoint, 160-165
        to spreadsheets, 158-159
        to Web sites, 166-169
    sounds to PowerPoint, 165
    text to Print House Magic, 171
Airbrush tool, 98
airbrushing glare, 98-99
albums. See photo albums
altering PowerPoint sample outline, 162
alternative color, 69
ArcSoft PhotoStudio Suite, installing, 16-19
Area Move tool, 67, 95, 119
aspect ratio, maintaining, 120-121
audio, adding to PowerPoint, 165
Auto button (Tone Adjustment dialog box), 93
Auto Launch (Kodak Picture CDs), 40
available disk space, determining, 4

B

backgrounds
    changing, 120-121
    cropping, 39
    PhotoFantasy
        inserting your picture in, 130-131
        selecting, 129
blending stitched images, 125
Bookmark Define dialog box, 81
bookmarking help pages, 81
borders (white), adding, 100-101
brightness
    adjusting Kodak DC240, 35
    images, 88-89
Brightness and Contrast command (Enhance menu), 88
Brightness and Contrast dialog box, Channel area, 89
brochures
    creating, 190-195
    fonts, 193-195
    images, importing, 192-195
    printing, 195
browsers, choosing, 45
Brush palette, 70
brushes
    Rate of Flow setting, 71
    selecting, 70
Bucket Fill tool, 70
buttons
    Add Attachments, 154-155
    Auto (Tone Adjustment dialog box), 93
    Change Info, 43
    Circle, 96-98
    Crop Tool, 87
    Done, 39
    Save Pictures Elsewhere on Your Computer, 41
    Select All, 37

C

calendars, creating, 182-185
Camera Setup, Kodak DC240, 34-35
cameras. See digital cameras
cards
    claim, 43
    picture, 36-37

cascading images, 55
CD-ROM
    image bank, 48-49
    included with book
        NetObjects Fusion, 26-31
        PhotoStudio Suite, 16-19
        Print House Magic, 20-25
    Presentation Backgrounds folder, 48
    WebGraphics folder, 48
Change Info button, 43
changing fonts in Web sites, 168
Channel area (Brightness and Contrast dialog box), 89
Circle button, 96-98
claim cards, 43
Clear command (Edit menu), 75
clearing selections, 75
Clipboard, 74
Close (X) button, 45
Close command (File menu), 82
closing
    albums, 145
    DOS window, 45
    images, 82
CMYK color, 78-79
color
    active, 69
    alternative, 69
    bucket fills, 70
    CMYK, 78-79
    gamma values, 79
    gradient fills, 70
    monitor configuration, 12
    RGB, 68, 78-79, 89
    selecting Color palette, 68
    transparency, 71
Color palette, 68, 96
color-calibrating printers, 78-79
commands
    Edit menu
        Add Frame, 100
        Clear, 75
        Copy, 74
        Cut, 75
        Paste, 74
        Stitch, 124
        Undo, 72
    Effects menu
        Emboss, 113
        Fine Art, Film Grain, 106
        Fine Art, Sketch, 105

Edit Text dialog box

Q-R

S